Ritchie Felix,
Copyright by Ritchie Felix

1

The Street Millionaire

By

Ritchie Felix

Table of Content

Be In Business for Yourself

Introduction:

With the boundaries that marked geographical definition of Nations submitting to the force of globalization, it is only wise for individual who hope to continue existence in this knowledge-driven Age to wake up from their mental stupor to appreciate the realities of the 21st century. We are living right now in the harshest of all time since the creation of this ontological void-"PLANET EARTH". Most well taught economic theories have failed with time and new ones are fast replacing them. Going to school to obtain great certificate do not guarantee best job as before since the jobs are not there.

It is wise to get your mine ticking and ticking rightly with a work that shows you the way out of this status to open you up imaginatively and create thought-provoking imagery that will release your mind from much burden. "**The Street Millionaire**" is an intellectual hype of the greatest order that will sweep you off your feet and connect you to the reality of hall of greatness of some sort that is not common with 21st Century. The pages of this book drips with pearls of gold and juices of intellectual wizardry of the mind of an uncommon Sage rising in the literary cosmos of the 21st century. Read with joy and pass on to your dear ones.

Ritchie Felix

Dedication

I dedicate this book to my Dear uncle Engr. Peter .E Ojugo, who picked me up amidst chaos and hopelessness in my tender age. He provided me with the shoulders of a giant on whom I stand today to rule my world. And also; to Chief (Mrs.) Sarah Nee Nwankwo kalu Ola of the blessed memory. How I wish you were here to see this epoch-making you started some decade ago in my life. Great Mother, I missed you really much.

CHAPTER ONE

The Making of 21st Century Millionaire.

❖ The Street University of Life swell with uncommon knowledge that is required to create millionaires out of thin air. Formal Universities have rolled out several graduates who have the best certificates around but not the best lifestyle in terms of finances. This is not a clever attempt to undermine the wisdom and hierarchy of intelligence oozing from these pristine varsities. <u>The truth must be told in clear words that our universities are yet to imbibe financial education leading to personal wealth creation and subsequent financial freedom into the academic curriculum</u>.

This could be termed a sort of mistake in a sense, but a closer examination of the order of things; one will easily observed that the school system majors much more on equipping the student to be an employee all through his life on earth. That is if the said job do not varnish into the void with time. Globalization has made it possible for jobs to migrate abroad leaving many skilled and unskilled persons handicapped of source of living.

A. **What do they teach you in the College?** - When jobs are fast disappearing into the tiny void, it is a normal thing for people to scramble after it and possibly migrate with it to keep body and soul together? <u>The School system do not prepare student on how to combat the adverse economy of recession or depression, or even give the fundamentals on how to handle personal unemployment, under-employment and over-employment.</u> The students are usually given skills to dodge risks and manipulate known formulas to solve mathematical equations problems. This might be debatable to an extent, yet, the truth therein cannot be denied by the end of the day.

Some hard mathematical problems will require multiple formulas to handle it, but this is not same as life problems. <u>The formulas to handle life problems are better taught and learnt on the streets of life. This is informal education you can call it.</u>

It is obvious in several parts of the World, students of formal Universities works for the graduates of the street university. The difference is just clear outside the school walls. The best graduates of any University are not necessarily the people who occupy the front row of fortune 500 Hall of fame. What is missing in our University education across the globe is financial education such that can help students of "Life University" to eke out living with ease and be in business to work for own income system. <u>Education is very important to survive in life, especially university education, but on the long run after school you discover to your chagrin that it is not everything. It can be a good tool to</u>

<u>start life with and not what to be depended upon on the long run.</u>

To be in business for yourself and mint your own money is the clarion call of the 21st century. You have the opportunity and right to swap terrains- from the Wall Street market place to high street market places. In recession or depression the walls of Wall Street economy surely come down crumbling into tiny pieces, but those who are on high streets economic parlance keep moving against the melting torrents. **How to survive adverse economic crunch is not taught**

in our school, rather it is how to survive with a certificate that every student has up his sleeves. <u>What is the relevance of certificate in the absence of jobs?</u> This is a "Teeth for Tat", and a good question at that, that will help you re-educate yourself if possible.

B. SECURITY FACTORS TO WATCH IF YOU MUST BE A MILLIONAIRE.

♦ **Job Security Vs Financial Security: -** One school teaches you to work very hard to earn money, while the other teaches you to employ money to work hard for you. This two paradigm realities have produced on the long run three identical triplets as follows:-

1. <u>**First one**</u> knows how to look for job, attend interviews and work very hard to earn money, and then turn over his financial security into the hands of Government or stranger who is the employer to handle for him. <u>He is trained in the formal university to avoid risks, and</u>

<u>even the risk to chart his own</u>
<u>very course for financial security.</u>

The word: SMART means to him to be very diligent at work and walking the corporate ladder to earn fat and fatter salary and allowances. He never considers this thought: if the owner of the ladder will wake up on the bad side one morning and decide to remove his ladder or people on his ladder. Even natural disaster can break the ladder and every one will come crash landing to zero economy. <u>Adverse</u> <u>economic conditions like</u>

<u>recession or depressions have shown several buoyant firms and conglomerate the way to zero economy</u>. They declared bankruptcy and went into extinction.

2. **The Second fellow** knows that be in a job just mean one is over broke beyond the skin of his wallet. He gets his high school education and college degree, but set out to make history for himself. He may be the genius on the academic block while in school, but he owns his own scripts to rule his world and be in business for himself. He unlearns himself of the garbage tugged into his mind by the school professors to take his acts to the next level in life.

<u>This fellow addresses problems by its context and not by any stereotyped formula given to him by the school teacher. He sees problems as challenges and as raw materials to deliver his brain children lurking deep within him</u>. Unlike his first brother, he understands the **dynamics of time** and **change** in the affairs of life. Also, he

know that life is not just about going to school, getting a high paying job, save money and invest in stocks and mutual funds. Some how, he perceives the deceit hidden within the entire system because his school professor is yet to tell him why he is not a millionaire and financially independent.

However, if being a millionaire or attaining financial independent is about good certificates and good job- then, his professors at Harvard, Princeton and Kings Colleges would have had been stinking Billionaires. These guys are among the smartest people around the education block that the world could boast to have, but are only helping to churn out graduates like government fire woods to keep the flames of executive slavery burning without a halt.

3. The Third Fellow: - is a confused, hopeless and helpless brother, junketing from one pole to the other while two brothers competes for who usurp leadership of the community. You can call this brother: "Middle class" who will be wiped off soon to make space for two world orders- the Rich and The poor **or very poor**. You can actually tell which is your security base from the school you attended so far. You can still make a choice if you discover that you are on the wrong voyage set out for a soon-to-be shipwreck.

C. 2 critical factors every millionaire must consider:

- **Employee   versus Entrepreneurship:** - The School curriculum design is in some way a weapon of mass destruction. In my book: "**Motivation for young people**" I did criticize the government for missing six all important links in the school curriculum design that has been the source of poverty in our society. The formal Education curriculum Design in so many ways did not teach a child the way to survive outside certificate economy.

The student graduates from one level to another till they come face to face with the reality of financial challenge. <u>It is then, that, they come to terms with the fact that they did missed out on something more precious on the issue of money in the classroom</u>. Even at the MBA executive classes, students are still loaded with much more garbage that cannot translate itself into the needed financial education that can guarantee financial security. Who designed the curriculum is a serious question any sane mind should ask? What exactly was the purpose or target hoped to achieve with this design is another?

It is important to find real answers to the questions above to enable you decipher the two world orders existing in every society. The world of employees and the golden world of entrepreneurs. Those who earn living by working for money only discover their stupidity late enough that they could only resign to fate and eventually die unfulfilled in life. <u>They had traded their energy, knowledge, time and other precious resources climbing another ladder</u>

<u>without minding their real business in life</u>.

Working for yourself is the real business in life, and working on yourself is another, but should be your preoccupation. The owners of the Banks, firms and companies they did worked for get so rich while they are not. Why? They were employees, and the later employers (i.e. Entrepreneurs). The entrepreneur works for solid profit by using **other people money, (OPM)** and **time** to eke out financial security for himself and his generation. On exit, the company is transferred to his children who continue to milk fortune from already established pipelines of crude wealth. <u>The employee on exist bequeath stretched poverty to his children because his certificates cannot be transferred to another. Its value dies same time the man who owns it die. His children re-enters the rat-race to re-invent the wheel to do same thing as their father.</u> This way the vicious cycle continues to plunder our Nation with much more miserably poverty.

My friend Martha by name, a freelance consultant in business development and management, also involve in corporate re-branding and personal coaching; once told me of a retired woman banker who engaged her services as a personal coach. She said to me that, the woman confided in her about the greatest mistake of her education and mind programming which made her spent all her precious time working for a bank whose gratuity is fast disappearing in less than five years after her retirement. <u>It was obviously life spent on magic grail sands of time</u>

<u>and space devoid of its physical monetary equivalent in both equity and time.</u>

On the 26th June, 2010, I sat on the panel that recruited staff-workers for fortune path limited- a multi level marketing company in Nigeria Sub-Sahara Africa. I discovered to my greatest surprise that more than 90% of people who came for the interview section asked to be employed as Office staffs, only 1.5% asked for field work to enable them earn passive income.

Among those who want office staff appointment are graduates with college degrees in both social sciences and pure sciences and few O. Levels. To help them face reality financially, I advised the company to issue a post-dated cheque of 200,000 Naira (i.e. Dollar equivalent of $1333.33) each for those who wanted office job, and leave them with these worlds: "If you can turn in two investors for the company -you earn N2000.00, and hundred per each investors. You can cash the cheque in your hand". I made them to understand that, the cheque can be cash any time-that is not necessarily by month end. You set your own target or salary and determine when to cash it- that is the simplest way to spell entrepreneurship.

I watched with stern surprise as these folks scrambled to grab the offer because the veil of slavery covering their eyes has been removed.

Many employees out there on the street are working on jobs that they do not like because it does not guarantee a future and financial security on the long run. Several folks hangs on because they want to earn their gratuity benefits, others hang on for the sake of job security, and millions others are just confused and cannot tell why they hang on- on a job that is nothing to write home about.

D_1. <u>Salary Vs Service</u>:-

Employees works very hard to

earn salary; entrepreneurs creates products or services to earn passive income which culminates on the long run into financial security and the man can retire or leverage into other things. <u>Salary economy tied up to line of dependants can do but nothing because it is stretched beyond its elastic limit. This way many employees across the poles of the universe continue to berth in the relegation waters of miserable poverty</u>. You can appreciate this reality better if you visit some parts of African. An employee in the metropolis sends money consistently to relations in the village from his monthly pay check. African culture celebrates extended family practice. This is great, especially if you are the receiver of aids from family members. But on the other hand, a grave burden on the shoulders of those this responsibility falls upon. The school system program student for financial limitation in that it reduces all the ingenuity, skills and talents, in the individual to just a paper qualification.

In the Industrial age then, the paper qualification can give you a good job, lofty lifestyle and help one keep some good reserves for the old age, but not now in the 21st century. The boundaries of things have been shifted over-board, and new speed limits are being set now-almost every hour that goes by. Yet, the school system has not changed even one bit.

Some old-curriculum still runs in the system and students are being given same old and cheap advice to study hard, get a good certificate or paper qualification and get a well paying job to invest in their retirement. <u>Blank Paradox! It is a development crime to run ones life with a typewriter mindset in the internet Age.</u> It is much more a treasonable felony to run a school system that addresses the challenges of expired reality in a much more developed socio-economic paradigm of the 21st century. It could not have been a sheer ignorance or mistake on the parts of those responsible for our school system. Rather, I strongly perceive sublimed deceit running in the system to keep the poor poorer and the rich richer. This is because, some of these folks if not all, do not have their wards in our schools. Their wards are sent abroad to get something better, more sophisticated and relevant to the reality on ground at the moment.

D. School System revolves around salary dynamics: - The School system focus students on the dynamics of salary. Each scheme in the curriculum is geared towards giving the individual skill to be better equipped at serving his employer better, and climb the corporate ladder at ease. This means the individual earns better salary the higher he goes up the ladder. <u>Salary lacks the efficacy to secure financial security for the individual on the long run, except the person is smart to invest his money in a lucrative portfolio that creates consistent cash flow.</u>

E. Salary is definite and Powerless before inflationary economic climate.

F. Salary scheme is a short-term approach to a life time challenge

G. Salary cannot make you gain financial independent rather helps you sink deep and deeper in dangerous depth. Debt becomes much more dangerous if the employee borrows money in advance waiting to pay back on the arrival of his pay check at the month end.

[

H. Salary economy cannot make millionaire out of anybody, except the individual buy into the world of entrepreneurship to create passive and residual income to augment his pay check.

I. **Salary scheme** is the <u>worst dynamics in distribution of National resources; equity and capital because, it empowers those who work less atop the corporate ladder, and disempowered the hard workers at the bottom of the corporate ladder.</u>

J. **Salary scheme** distorts perspective, misplaces National priority and surely under-develop the society because on the long run it discourages entreprenualism. The wealthy of any developed Nation is direct result or import of entrepreneurs' activities.

Entrepreneurship creates cash flow into the country by developing products and services which people and companies exchange for money or its prototypes.

D₂. SERVICE DYNAMICS

While doing my executive degree course with the Applied Scholastic

International I learnt that there are several barriers to learning that makes it difficult for some people to actually practice what they have learnt in school. One of them is **misunderstood word or concept**. A concept is not understood properly by a student if there be a word in the definition or explanation of the concept that he did not understand. This evolves into a misunderstood concept and if nothing is done by his instructor or coach to clear the misunderstood word by process of word clearing, then like **a tiny grenade the misunderstood word or concept can metamorphosed into a ballistic missile by shattering the reality of**

the subject being taught. This way people have not been able to underscore the exact differences between ones **profession** and **own business**. Your profession is not your business and vice versa.

i.   Your profession gives you salary as reward for the services you render to another that profits on the long run.

ii.   Your business gives you real income either as passive or residual income, and this income is infinite in nature. It is reward for the services you render to yourself that gives equity even in the future.

iii. Your business generates either products or services that create cash flow in the form of pay check, book royalties, license royalties, rentage income, stock dividends and others.

iv. Your business is what will make you rich and give you financial security at the end of the day.

It is important to note here, that your business create income opportunities for others. Who are your team members to help in generating your products or services? The opportunity to learn from others is there and you can as well leverage on the platform of each team member if you are a good net worker. You do not need to raise a sales pitch to do that. You just have to go about it professionally. This is what I call "developing the businesses in your business". I will throw more highlight on this in later chapters of this work. Your products or services keep you in business by consistent generation of cash flow.

CHAPTER TWO

WHAT YOUR PROFESSOR DID NOT TEACH YOU AT HARVARD BUSINESS SCHOOL

The School System drill students to develop the mindset for capital gains instead of focusing them to develop quest for cash flow. The Street Millionaire do not have passion for capital gains rather shop for businesses or deal that can constantly bleed other people pockets to swell his bank account on a regular basis. Capital gain mindset is the quest behind job-driven persons in the society. It is one of the major disadvantages of the school system or its curriculum design. The universities are supposed to be a citadel where students are naturally transformed into shrewd entrepreneurs who place much more priority on cash flow than on capital gains. The government security bond, stocks, mutual funds, hedge fund and retirement funds- all runs on the dynamics of capital gain. Only few entrepreneur minded persons approaches these investment portfolio with cash flow mindset.

In the business school, you are encouraged to invest for long term (i.e. for capital gain), but on the street smart children invest for the short term as long as profits accrues to the portfolio. The street millionaires believe in given his money the right velocity to keep it in motion and in steady generation of cash flow. The business school is silent about cash flow whether it is for ignorance or for a clever purpose only time will time and unravel how the richest people in the system uses the curriculum design to keep the unsuspecting masses stranded and poverty-stricken in the long run. Right now, if you have eyes- you will observe that several economic theories and hypotheses by our Honourable professors in our Universities are getting expired in both content and reality by the day. The rapidity of change and the speed of technologically innovation have rendered many economic theories or Doctoral dissertation obsolete. It is a crime of our school system today to continue to feed unsuspecting students with garbage of expired reality. Barrack Obama is the President of United States of America and George W. Bush is also a President of USA is not same in logic, though literally it might strike a chord or a note of symphony. George W. Bush was a President of USA- that is an expired reality. The man Obama is the Present reality. It is important our school professors score the card of difference between an expired curriculum design and the current.

This must be done rightly in both design and practice to encourage students to make shift in perspectives in regard to their financial life. Emphasizing so much on the need for job security or investing for the long term or for capital gains is the cheapest way to show people pathway to fiery furnace of miserable poverty. Education should be education and not indoctrination. There is urgent need for our school professors to unlearn themselves of the bitter advises of the industrial Age and embrace the efficacy of the present global reality.

Our School and public libraries need to be de-bugged of expired text books and resource materials. Or at least marked them boldly with the inscription: "EXPIRED". This will at least help the user to use the information in them with caution. Imagine what happens when a student is roll out of the university crucible on expired knowledge template to face the realities of the 21st Century, he surely is a gross misfit by all standards. It does not matter the name of the school or portfolios of its professor for so long the baking materials employed in weaning him through the system is faulty, he is already expired ever before he is graduated from the school academic oven.

Little wonder, many are getting poor and poorer by the day. Marriages are hitting shipwrecks of divorce for reasons bordering on finances or lack of it. The bricks of over primordial values are fast crashing down daily into pieces before us at the centre stage that once held all together cannot hold again. The school system of the expired paradigm reality has done more harm than good at the present.

MONEY LITERACY-CATALYST FOR WEALTH CREATION IN WISDOM AGE

The degree of poverty in the cast two decades is mind bulging, and this is a significant pointer to the fact, that the school system programmed us to think in the terms of language, therefore we cannot conceptualize in real material terms what we do not have language to describe. This is the convention that has been prevalent among us for years. Somehow it gives definite portrait picture of what we esteem as reality.

Now, the school does not offer any minor or major course on money education, we therefore lack the insight and the ultimate language to command money because in the first place we are handicapped of its actual concepts. Every course has a language or jargon, if you are acquainted with its language; naturally you command the dynamics of its concepts. On the other hand, if you are ignorant of the right language, you surely be either E-grade or F-grade student of the 21st century has unveiled the degree of decay in our financial education or the obvious lack of it. Money literacy is the catalyst that accelerates ninth creation anywhere in the world. It is a universal principle that is old as the universe itself, and works independent of personal socio-economic status or religious affiliation. It is as real as the periodic principle of time and laws of Universal gravity.

+ Financial Education breeds financial intelligence which is far better than any other faculty when it comes to wealth creation. There are several faculties that are called into play when wealth creation is involved. The conventional way is to go higher on the corporate ladder to earn huge amount of money as pay check monthly. This is considered high level of smartness on the academic block, but I think it is a preconceived error running in our system. This pattern of error has sent many unsuspecting souls to their untimely grave whenever events turns table around.

The corporate ladder here could be leaning on a wrong wall and the wall could collapse one day, then, every theory and thesis will prove abortive. Or even the owner of the ladder could decide suddenly to dismantle his ladder from the wall or sell it over to another who might not be willing to keep folks on it standing or climbing. It is a wrong financial mindset or rather faculty to equate wealth creation to academic ingenuity or attainment. Some smarter kids on the school block can decide to diversify their investment portfolio but on wrong platforms. That eventually strips them of the last dime when they needed it most for security.

Financial Literacy helps you understand the dynamics and mechanics of creating steady cash flow from your investments despite the challenge of any economic crisis. Your University Professor will tell you to save money, but will not teach you what inflation will do to your effort to create wealth. The school will teach you to invest your money wisely for the long term for capital gains, but will not teach you how inflation catches up with the funds in the bank. The business school will teach you to be smart enough to diversify your investment into different portfolios, but will not teach you how to leverage on it to create consistent cash flow in the face of adverse economic agitation. Money literacy is everything in wealth creation no matter the economic crisis of the day.

MONEY LITERACY- CATALYST TO ATTAINING FINANCIAL FREEDOM

The rate of unemployment, job loses and poverty is alarmingly on the increase. As an employee in the present global reality, chances are that in the near future or by a flip of change on the radar of technology, you will either resign, retire or get retrenched. One out of these three is bound to happen.

Consequently, what steps or strategies are you engaging to ensure that for the rest of your life, you do not die in miserable poverty or consider re-entering the job market at your retirement; but end your journey as satisfied, wealthy personality and live the rest of your days in affluence of financial security?

Albeit, you may not be able to turn back the hands of time to make desired changes; such is only possible in Holy wood Movies starring Angelina Jolie in

Tomb Raiders. It is imperative you draw up enough strength from within the Trinity of your body, soul and spirit to launch ardent campaign against poverty and financial insecurity by becoming financial literate at all cost. Money literacy is very important and is everything in helping you attain financial freedom at the end of the day.

4. **HOW TO BECOME FINANCIAL LITERATE:** Hopefully many unsuspecting students run to do their MBAs in the University business schools to get smarter financially ahead of their contemporaries; little wonder, their very soul is further stuffed to full capacity with garbage of expired convention of failed economic theories. What a holocaust!

Let me say this in stern words, that, the MBA courses are really wired to enable students achieved job security, not financial security. To achieve financial freedom you need not to work for another for a long time. If working for another is that much important at least to test your professional prowess and see what it is like being in the corporate setting, then, work to learn and not to earn.

Learning empowers more than earning in the long run. The former is infinite in dividend while the later is finite or limited. Whatever you learn while working for another can be duplicated by you over time to tinker your own business in the right direction for optimum profits.

Again, you need to read good books on financial education, especially the ones written by successful self-made millionaires or entrepreneurs having empirical evidences for their mastery of money concepts over the years. Buy their tapes to listen while on the move, attend their coaching classes or even go for private consultation. This will only cost you a dime. But equip you with right tool kits to face your world and lance out a great fortune for yourself.

It is suicidal to attempt going into business just with what you gathered from the business school. You have very slim chance to just survive and be in business with clutches of challenges beyond measure. You can save yourself this headache by picking up a Coaching DVD, Tape, Online Coaching

Ritchie Felix,
Copyright by Ritchie Felix

Classes or One-on-One live Coaching in the area of your business idea by the hands of a money guru having real live records to back up his status. Here, I can recommend for you RICH-Dad Cash flow Board games or Classes to help you take your money game to the next level of reality. Understanding the language of money makes you commander of wealth and be in money beyond the "dialogismos" (Greek word for Imagination) of the universe.

5 REASONS WHY HARDWORKING PEOPLE END IN POVERTY.

North-South, East-West and round the globe, there are men and women who have had more than a fair share of the wealth cornucopia of the universe. On the other hand, some people have had more problems than you could imagine. Despite the fact, that our world at present-parade self made millionaires who are in wheel chairs, who are blind, deaf and mentally retarded or even declared uneducable, yet, whenever the roll call is taken, more men and women who are noticeably working very hard ends up in devastating poverty. Why? It is the question that our school curriculum is yet to provide adequate answer for.

Right now, it is important we explore the five reasons behind people impoverishment despite unending effort to get things better:

+ **INABILITY TO THINK ABOUT RETIRING WEALTHY:-**

It is common to hear a Professor in the business school talk about retiring wealth. Their emphasis majors on the retirement plan like 401(K), hedge fund, mutual fund and all that lofty government retirement security programs. Either by sheer omission or error commission, directly or indirectly, they will not inform you in the MBA classes that a little bib on the radar of technology or shifting on the National Economic scale or even outright paradigm shift in global economic matrix can thwart the ability of the Government to keep to the promises of that security plan. This way; many have gone into poverty for lack of back up

Plan "B" or not thinking retiring wealthy on a personal effort.

Inability to think about retiring wealthy is the mother of all poverty of all poverty in the land right now. Many men and women work very hard to help the government or their employer make ends-meet and gain the future, but fail woefully to plan for a wealthy retirement in the near future. My greatest fear now is what happens to this bunch in the face of Major National or Global Economic Crisis?

WORK FOR JOB SECURITY INSTEAD OF WORKING

TOWARD FINANCIAL SECURITY: - To work hard for money makes miserable and a future at the end of the day. Several men and women across the globe are working on the job they hate with passion but for the sake of job security. Others had enough to get appraisal and climb higher on the corporate ladder but without thinking to retire rich and have financial security. Yet some, work for the name of the company. Some people work for the annual benefit plan or quarterly benefit plan, which ever bracket you belong nothing empowers like minding your own business to take of the future.

- **PROCRASTINATE OR POST-PONED RETIREMENT TILL AT VERY OLD AGE:-** This is a grievous crime many are committing against themselves and against posterity. At 50-55Yrs so many men and women are still actively engaged working for money. Approaching the golden age of immortality (i.e. between 55-65 Yrs), they begin to discover the frantic turn of events against what they had expected. But the reality is that They cannot do much with this limited time and space, they just discovered that they had delivered destinies into the hands of strangers with empty promises. What an ordeal!

There is no need working in the first if the future is not guaranteed. It is obvious that he employer is out to scoop profit for his investment, and not to take you to your financial Eldora do. It is useless procrastinating or keep push your day of resignation into an unknown date in the future.

Right now, the age is in your favour and the raw energy is still there. You have to rise now to sack your Boss or face the music later in the future. As an employee today, chances are that in the near future, you resign, retire or get retrench. One out of these is bound to happen. It is only a tree that will wait until it is cut down before it gives way.

I was once there on the corporate ladder, doing the hardest part of the job for my organization. I won for myself several promotions and awards that never translate into financial security. I used to be a strong fanatic of job security and never want to hear someone talk about resigning or going into business for you. I had all my eggs in one basket till the bubble burst in the stock market affect my organization badly and the rest was stories. I did resign the hard way and face the reality of the insecurity of joblessness. I almost lost my family in the process. You see, it is not the best way to learn by experience. I therefore urge you to borrow leaf from experience and take a rethink at your Job right now. What is the guarantee that you will stay on this job in the next five years, ten years or more? What is the guarantee that the lofty retirement packages promised will be delivered to you automatically just as planned? Do you have a second plan to outwit your employer or the apparent turns of events should equations go out of balance? You have to properly informed up to the minute less you plunge your destiny into the tiny air.

+ **INABILITY TO DELAY GRATIFICATION:-**

Failure is usually a plan event by some people. By the way they approach life generally points to this fact. They are very poor handlers of money. They cannot delay selfish gratification a minute so long there is money to spend. These kinds of people are usually the worst victims of sales pitch in the media and on newspaper headlines. By their consistent action and way of handling finances – they program themselves to fail in life and disappoint the expectation of those who had hoped in them.

This is not a case of not being able to make money, rather not be able to keep money. Naturally, they build companies, hospitals and erect car garage in their stomachs. Take to x-ray them; you see great building, well equipped hospitals and fleet of cars sitting in their bowels. What is supposed to develop the asset column of their balance sheet is already eaten into the stomach. What a bad way to live.

Our school system do not tell us that every impulse buy program us for failure with 90% probability. Of course, the curriculum somehow encourages the student to allow cash flowing from his pocket into another just to satisfy his craze not real need. Some people buy stocks for the sales pitch of the salesman, and not for creating cash flow. Other go into slavery of poverty consciously by accepting loans upon loans which creates ever expanding hole on their credits. This way another takes them into captivity by making merchandize out of them.

DO NOT UNDERSTAND THE DISAPPONINTMENTS OR APPOINTMENTS BEHIND FINANCIAL STATEMENTS: -

The accounting system taught in our schools does not help the student to actually apply the knowledge gained to ascertain their financial future. It is important to know that behind every financial statement given to you or published in the media or on papers there is an encrypted message within. Each figure commands either an appointment with credit or disappointment with debit.

The students are always encouraged to balance their balance sheet but such is not usually obtainable in real life setting. It is either you are in liability of some sort or you have great assets streaming with cash flows. Whenever, your asset column balances against your liability, then, you are still struggling with your finances. If the Assets are greater, then, for sure- you are in money, and if the opposite- you are on a rat race move-running away from your creditors.

For academic purpose, you can fine-tune your balance sheet to strike a balance, but never in the real life.

Inability to understand from the financial statements of companies whether public or private the state of things in the economy is a direct way to head the wrong direction. Several men and women who are working very hard rarely find time to read the news dailies or listen to the media. To read the financial journals or the publication of Wall Street Economy is an odd thing to do by some folks. Even if the read such, they cannot understand or pay less attention to the statistics of the financial statements. They cannot decode the pointer of the economy from such publications, and surely head in the wrong direction in the near future. What happen later makes the headlines for the news in the future.

If you will not fail the expectation of loved ones on you,

then, you have to take stock of what is responsible for your financial mishaps now. This way you beat the pangs of poverty in the near future. It is far cheaper in both time and actual cost to live in knowledge, than to stay glued to your ignorance. Success and failure is both plan even you have a choice to make. Choose success!

TOPIC: THE DEBT RESERVE OF FEDERAL RESERVE

What is usually taught in our schools about the central bank, the Government and Federal Reserve is quiet insignificant to the actual business or operations of these entities. On the academic block the text books and classes are structured in such a way that students develop strong affinity to work for any of these institutions without questioning who the actual owners are. All of the world, two out of the three or even all are owned by some invisible cabals who plunder the wealth of the masses to stay on top of the economy of the day. These ones are completely immune from the fangs of the biting economy by the way of legal framework sustaining the structures.

This is the simple reasons behind the underdevelopment of most third world countries of the world. The cabals at the apex makes merchandize of the masses using the legal instruments enshrined in National constitutions. At the onset of the global economic melt down in 2007, many countries opted for a bailout to stabilize the economy,-large funds were plunged into the system with the camouflage to save the economy, but indirectly melt the cash value of the savers money in the bank. It was the bailout that actually sunk the last hope of many unsuspecting masses whose liabilities hit the high heavens.

In most developed countries, the bailout further widened the gap between the rich and the poor of the society. The rich actually become richer by the bailout exercise while the poor get poorer to a stench. At this, much debt was introduced into the system by those who run our banks and financial institutions. The poor masses are saddled with the responsibility to pay off this huge indebtedness introduced by the government via the CBNs and the Federal Reserve.

At this, it is wise to question what is the status of the "Reserve" of the Federal Reserve for the American People and for the world at large. The Dollar is global reserve currency and anything that affects it affects the world at large. If the money in our CBNs are debts and of course disaster is waiting to happen, then, what about the "Reserve" of the Federal Reserve? Someone is up with a funny game, and doing everything possible to deceive the masses with fast flips of Economic slang. The more of such jargons, the deeper we sink down into the quagmire of debts.

The turns of events in 2010 starting the year with streams of Earthquakes, landslide and unending economic crisis points back to history of two centuries gone. Then, it was wars, new discoveries and the beginning of new economic era. In the 21st Century, it is different thing altogether, but in all pointing to a time of greater economic crisis that virtually will redefine the trinity of time, space and standard of living, or way of living in both content and reality of its concepts. The whole world is enmeshed into a time of travail like a pregnant woman. At the end of the day, the middle class will be completely wiped out give way for the two world orders: The rich and the very poor.

❖ **ERA OF MISERABLE POVERTY:-**
This is not a prophecy of any sort because the indices are glaring enough before us today. The Federal Reserve in real term has nothing in its Reserve for the world or for the American people. The CBNs of the world cannot perform any magic; instead coagulate the

system with much more of its poisonous derivatives.

In Nigeria, before the bailout of #400 Billion by Mallam Sansui the CBN Governor, the economy was a bit better than what obtains at the moment in the country. By the time the bailout was offered to some selected banks in 2009, several stocks have melted to even zero in the market; The Nigerian case is more or less the worse case scenario as over 60% of investors in the stock market are net financial literates. They had come into the market because of the sales pitch of stock brokers or its agents in various banks. I can recall back the incidence that took place somewhere in the Western part of the country while on tour for seminars on financial education. Those expected to be in one of the meetings by my agents did not show up until the last day of the seminar. One of them stood to and decried how the banks in their neighborhood through its agents persuaded them in workshop session to invest now into the stock market. The young man regretted that, had he heard about this teaching on financial education, he would not have been easily and cheaply deceived to cast his lots into the stock market.

The financial institutions around are usually own by the rich and mighty either the economy or in the political corridors of power. The stock brokers and their agents works for this money bags and deceived the unsuspecting masses to turn in their wallets in their favour in a well organized scheme of investment. The people continued to languish in agony of pain and lost of hard earned money when the bubble came. This is a legal fraud supported by the government against the poor masses in the land.

All over the globe, the poor are the worst affected by this recent financial turmoil for the lack of financial literacy. The Paradox here; this people do not shop any interest at all to do something about getting right financial education. This way miserable is unleashed upon the people.

❖ WHO PAYS FOR THE BAILOUT MONEY?

Ordinary people expect the government or its agents to pay for the bailout largesse to banks and other preferred bodies. It is only a big joke because the poor of the land will pay for this via high taxes, bank charges, income tax and all that. This is why the money that is yet to be paid for the worker's salary is already debts on itself. The printed money has literally taken great value away from the money in the savings and salary of workers in the future.

Again as the inflation assumes a higher and unbearable dimension, the rich gets richer and richer by the day while the poor gets poor, poorer and dirty stinking poor. The bailout money will be paid even by the kids of the poor as they grow up amidst this cash heist of the 21st century. The way out of this orchestrated impoverishment is in getting financial education as the rich, and then joins them to play this game of monopoly. The poor plays this same game, but never thought of same working against him in real life. As innocent Junior high school student-monopoly and chase games were my best and favorite. Then, it meant only entertainment and tool for one to help sharpen his mind to speed up for high performance. But, as I grew up and observed the scheme of the rich against the poor, I knew this game is responsible for making few people own several firms or conglomerates, and employ the teeming population to work for them in order to earn living.

CHAPTER THREE

SUCCESS IN LIFE IS A GAME

As far as I am concerned, success is a game of choice each individual will make consciously, and prepare to work for to earn. It does not answer to hard work or smart work devoid of financial intelligence. Only few people hit the gallery of success by hard work and still stay success. The number is less than 1% in actuality.

SIX SMART WAYS TO BECOME SUCCESS AND STAY RICH IN 21ST CENTURY

❖ **GET KNOWLEDGE: -** In the industrial age, paper certificate was equated to money. In the present information age, knowledge is money. The key to attain success the smartest way is to acquire useful knowledge. It is this kind that is equated to power and money respectively. However, knowledge is power only when such knowledge is useful, applicable, valuable and convertible into money or its prototype. Therefore, not all knowledge equates to money. It is only knowledge that is relevant, useful, valuable, applicable or convertible into raw cash that is power.

The level of reward any knowledge will command in the marketplace depends on its usefulness or perceived value in any given geo-political entity. The more useful and convertible your knowledge is the more money it can generate for you or whoever engages it. The most in-demand stock of the 21st century is useful knowledge that has capacity to add value to either individuals or to corporate bodies, or even both. If you have what the world, with their cash in their hands, they beat a foot-path to your door post regardless of where you are in the world.

You have to develop your own knowledge products or services, and package it properly to meet the needs of the market if you want to be a success. Bill Gates, Michael Dell, Robert Kiyosaki, IBM Corporation, Ted Turner, Jeff Bozos, Oprah Winfrey, Steve Wozniak and Steve Jobs, etc, are all toping the chart of the world Billionaires for their uncommon mental imports targeted to both individuals and corporations across the globe.

Financial education will help you think in terms of knowledge and provision of services to the society for the satisfaction of felt needs and wants of many even beyond borders. This way, you activate the inflow of riches into your life. To this end, your best ever principal investment in life is to acquire useful knowledge that empowers you to create and add value (wealth) to the world.

❖ Get Advice from those experienced in the field of your specialty or field you choose to go into. Make no mistakes, life is not about competition. Your major assignment is not to get ahead of others or those in your choice field, but to get ahead of yourself. The school system programs students for competition in life, and that is the school issues certificates of honors to students. But, financial education unleashes financial intelligence to students, and do not program them for competition, rather tone their skills to attain self actualization that comes with financial security.

Little wonder, every student of financial education does not hesitate to ask for or give intelligent advises to others. His blessing is to only get ahead of himself and conquer his fears and limitations to become rich and superlative rich in life.

You need useful advice from people who have experiences that you need to move your game to the next level of manifestation- ask for advice from right people even if it cost you a dime- you need it to bridge the gap of trial & error or that of ignorance. Make no mistake to ask a stock agent or stock broker where to invest your hard earned bucks, less you get your fingers burnt off badly beyond recognition. Ask experienced investor with clear track record of success over the years. Do not forget this might cost you time or money or even both. For investment generally, I will prefer to ask the Rich Dad dude, and for selling- I will ask Brain Tracey, and for anything stock- I prefer Warren Buffet. Then for TV Show, I will ask Oprah Winfrey, and I can go on to mention millions of others. So long, I do not ask Ngozi

Okonjo Iwela of World Bank about Tomb-raiding when Lady Croft (Angelina Jones) is there.

❖ **INVEST IN CORE COMPETENCES**: - Successful people are not usually jack of all trades, master of none. The rich recline into the area of his lost fit, but the poor scampers after many things and at the end of the day, he lacks mastery of all. Do what you have flare for and naturally cut out for. The rich uses money to accomplish other things beyond his abilities. He becomes a success at the end of the day. As a beginner, the best way to start is to take inventory of your stock of specialize knowledge, skills, gifts and talents. Develop yourself very well in core areas to gain the exceptional competence that is required in making uncommon history of great success.

❖ **FORGET GET-RICH-QUICK IDEAS:** - In the school of financial intelligence cutting corners to join together later is a blatant felony. Financial literacy is not about undue smartness or ones ability to skip classes of useful life lessons. Rich people of the world knew from albinitio that financial independence is not about exotic cars, magnificent edifice, and ability to hire condo or cruise in a private yacht across the globe. The rich know it is about the value your products or services offers to humanity. And if the major subject here is humanity- you need not cut corners. Life generally abhors it and the societies do not celebrate get-quick-rich scheme or its millionaires. The best thing you need is to follow the existing modus operandi of doing things- that successful people had followed in the past to attained wealth and fortune. It works for you the same

Ritchie Felix,   107
Copyright by Ritchie Felix

result as it did for others in the past.

❖ **GET A PLAN OF ACTION: -** Nothing works for you until you make it work. You need a game plan in blue-print to gazette your daily, weekly and monthly activities that will take you into the universe cornucopia of wealth. Your plan should tell a story of your business goal, ideological standing and way to exist the rat-race to nib into the orb of your projected success. It is difficult to fail in life with facts and plan of action.

❖ **BE IN BUSINESS FOR YOURSELF:-** According to John Hancock; "The more people who own little business of their own, the safer our country will be, and the better off its cities and towns; for the people who have a stake in their country and their community are its best citizens"

The truth remains that nobody gets financial freedom by working for another. You have to be in business for yourself. Being in business success is not about luck; it is about applying principles to whatever you do. Time tested principles works independent of any inherent or external factors and irrespective of the status or social back of the person who apply it.

You can actually set up your own business, and take the first step towards breaking the yoke of eternal financial struggle that is the result of working for somebody else, all your life. When you set up a business run by yourself, you have only become self-employed you do not truly own a business yet. You only become a true investor and a business owner when you do not have to be part of the business set up for it to survive.

Owning a profitable business or business not run by you is a source of real income and stable supply of wealth. You can engage in other business or activities of great profits since you do have to be a part of your business for it to work. This will afford you the quality time to be with your family and friends. Even when you go away for months or years, your business do not suffer; rather it grows stronger and better by the day under competent management team. When you set up a business that is successfully managed by others, you have effectively combined people at work and money at work- method of wealth creation. That is a sure route to great fortune and super success.

❖ ONE GAME TWO SEPARATE RESULTS: - The rich and the poor have something in common in the name of the game both plays to be where they are separately in life. Since life is a stage, every one with a script either good or bad takes his chance to run his scripts. The rich and the poor have different scripts but play the same game, and come out with different results. The name of the game is in six letters and spell as ; "HABITS". It is the type of habit that each has that create the vast chasm separating the two in real life.

CHAPTER FOUR

TWELVE PRINCIPLES OF WEALTH CREATION

The effective combination of success habits with time tested wealth creation principles will make you roll in unending success and enable you retire early enough to swim in millions of money. From my research while putting this work together, I discovered these principles that I carefully outlined as follows:-

- **USE PROBLEMS AS RAW MATERIALS TO WORK OUT YOUR SUCCESS IN LIFE**: - The ordinary mind perceives challenges as problems are projects waiting to happen as success. The rich uses problems to make outstanding differences in life. If you must grow money and success with ease and without capital, you need to make use of personal and societal challenges to create a stable income stream for yourself. People pay you money for the problem you solve or your services or products offers to them. Street millionaires of the 20th and 21st century cashed on the opportunities in the womb of problems to become great and rule their world with treasures beyond measure.

Naturally, every financial scarcity is a pointer to hidden wealth somewhere in the womb of the cosmos. You need ideas innovative enough to release the money hibernating within your creative faculties. You need not get frustrated in the face of financial battle-necks, use your lack to draw inspiration of what kind of money you would want to have, your magnetized mind come to play; begin to paint the colour of your money on the walls of your imagination, put it on black and white, then write down at the least twenty things you can do legitimately to actualize the figures before you on the paper. If you are able to add reasonable action to your magic paper, then you are on your way to swim in super-abundance of money.

Again you may need to engage others who will buy into your business idea, but do not go solo as two good heads are better than one rotten brain.

- **START WITH WHAT YOU HAVE & WHERE YOU ARE IF YOU MUST MAKE HISTORY**:- To make the drawing on the paper is far easy than taking the plan off paper to actuality give it features to make history. Several dreams and good visions die naturally on the chalk board or white paper ever before they are taking off. You do not have to wait to have all that you need to start. You can start with the little you have or even with nothing right where you are, and watch history being made in the process of time. The most important things you need for a start one;

*   Clear cut vision

*   Innovative ideas

*   Healthy body

*   Courage and the ability to start up immediately. Every other thing is secondary. Much of what you need will naturally show up when you must have started out.

Approach business like a child in the womb. All the child needs to speak, to walk, hear and do everything are already in the tender cradle-tied in the mother's womb. The most important assignment of the "baby-child" is to break forth through the mother's uterus to be born alive, and then every other thing needed will show with time. You need not to keep postponing the date to start, just start, and you will be surprise you will not fall as you had presumed, but stand out to be a great success history in your neighborhood.

- **HAVE AN OWN PERSONAL SUCCESS CONCEPT**: - Create your own parameters to evaluate your success, and never make the mistake of seeing yourself in the very eyes of another. Write your own script and formula to attain success. Know exactly what you want, and how much you want it, and how you want to get it. It is a serious mistake many people out there on the street made that incapacitated the gem of genius in them.

Log into the deep within you engaging your creative faculties to write out what success means to your person-unique you in your own world. The people around you might address you or treat you base upon the immediate circumstances around you, but your true originality is who you real are in your own eyes and evaluations.

Ritchie Felix,
Copyright by Ritchie Felix

This will help you to define your own success in your own words and language. You know words are the tools of the mind that you can leverage on to be the man of your dream.

Words repeated over time gives a kind of attitude to the mind, and the magnetize mind is pre-conditioned to respond to certain language which revolves around or build its own concept which bears the reality of the individual. You need to coil out your own model of success. Every manifested genius has his own success model, module or template. You just need to know this on time to be the original in your world.

The School curriculum has taken lot of folks out of what they are naturally cut out for, and arms them with empty certificates. You don't have the way life has placed you after reading this masterpiece. Look for things to unlearn yourself of, and look for useful replacements to fortify your arts in wealth creation. You may be over-dress to access the kind of money you need, so get dress down and redress for the kind of money you want.

- **DON'T LOVE MONEY, BUT DON'T LACK IT:-** From Genesis to Revelation in the Holy Bible, prayer was mentioned only 500 times while money was mentioned 2,500 times because of its importance in the lives of men, and its significance in the program of God, especially for the last days. To have money is not the root of all evil but lack of it is a capital sin to both man and God.

God will not create money rather gave the intelligence behind its creation. Man created money out of quest to attain freedom and perfection, hence man created the universal principles governing money. You are not close to having money in abundance if you are behind or in T-grade of the study of its principles.

- **MONEY RESPONDS TO WORDS**:

- The words we speak to ourselves is very important, especially in wealth creation. Rich words produce rich mind and rich mind produce rich man; and same way poor words produce poor mind, and poor mind produce poor man. Words are the tools that fuel the brain to react negatively or positively. Words are the first capital you need in creating a befitting future, success and super-abundant money for yourself. It is you affirm positive words that come your way from others, and also instantly reject negatives words as they come to you. But most importantly, your own words speak to yourself is the most effective, efficient and efficacious in wealth creation or poverty creation. Money responds to words.

Positive words about money spoken overtime graduates or culminate into vocabulary that is on its own a unique money concept. Good money concept will indefinitely give you a special attitude and language about money which on the long run begins to interplay in your daily or minute's action. This way, you leverage yourself from poverty to a success and stay in unlimited supply of money. This is my unique formula for any willing soul, irrespective of background, skin colour, educated or not, with job or no job, and with capital or not that can help you create unlimited supply of money and stay very rich.

RULES GUIDING MONEY MAKING ON THE STREETS IN THE WISDOM AGE

i.   Money is remuneration for services rendered.

ii. Money comes in forms ideas, talent and natural gifts that can be sharpen to produce real cash flow.

iii. Ideas are travel at the speed of thought says Bill Gates, virtually over 50,000 thoughts (i.e. Sublimed ideas) passes through your minds every 24hr; these ideas are money spinners if you carefully, resourcefully and timely engage it to the process of conversion into its physical equivalents. This idea has the ability to intersect the cash flow of your country (i.e. currency in circulation) and bring it to your door step, to your office or home, street corner or bank account.

iv. Money is a reward for problem solved. If you want more money solve more problems.

v. Idea is what you need to tap into the cornucopia of wealth in the cosmos, and intersect the billions flowing through the internet.

vi. What you need to create your own money is not far from what is in your hand right now, either zero capital or venture capital. For if you can't be a Bill Gates, you can buy a software affiliate marker with ebay.com or amazon.com, and if you can't be a Michael Jackson, you can write lyrics or be the biggest studio drummer. If you can't be a good footballer, you can be the best hand on the goal post. You can even be the best lines-man or referee in the field. If you can't be a Jennifer Lopez, you can be Angelina Jolie or even a Brad Pitt, and if you can't be Obama Barrack of United States, you can be a Hillary Clinton- Secretary of State. A living dog is better than a dead lion. You just have to keep moving at all cost because even the planets will all its loads of stars is in constant motion. If you can't fly-run, and if you can't run, and if you can't walk-keep shaking yourself so that people will not mistakenly dump you into the mortuary supposing you are dead. Death is not your portion; success is your portion... even now!

vii. Quit speeding spree on liabilities like trendy fashion, fun fair, foods, cinemas, games, betting's, etc you will discover you have what it takes to start at your business venture.

viii. Money comes in forms of wages, dividends, royalties, rebates, and reward for services you render and return on good investment or equity.

- <u>DON'T LOOK FOR MONEY, CREATE IT:</u> - There is money everywhere but do not go looking for it, rather have money looking for with ultrasonic speed. The school system programs students to look for money by all means, but the universal law of wealth creation on the streets is to have money looking for you. How do you get money looking for you? The answer is simple and obvious- Create what money need and you surely see it splashing all over you like hailstones from above. Create your own product or service, and then you mint your own money.

- <u>MOVE AWAY FROM "RED OCEAN" TO "BLUE OCEAN"</u>:- In my book "Income Edge"- subtitled "Unveiling the most guided wealth creation principles (i.e. secrets) in difficult economic weather", I defined or rather explained "Red Ocean" as sectors, fields, careers or areas in life that people have already discovered, exploited and keep plundering; and "Blue Ocean" as unknowns undiscovered and uncluttered paths or economic and uncluttered paths or economic paradigms of life. There is much more competition in the "Red Ocean" of life now than ever because of 21st century global population explosion. But the waters of "Blue Ocean" are green and swell with opportunities.

You need to go through school to cash on the success or money in the "Red Ocean" of life because there exist already made universal rules. You do not need school to process your success and create your own money in the

"Blue Ocean" of life because you are the one who sets the rule for your products or services. To be in business for yourself and roll in millions of money in your street corner you need to move away from "Red Oceans" and leverage on the economy of "Blue Ocean" of life. Simply write your own scripts, build your own stage, create your own ladder, set your own rules and Rule your world by surprise! Glow and go mobile with your dream beyond the "dialogismos" of the universe

Ritchie Felix,
Copyright by Ritchie Felix

and be "Makarios" (blessed) with "Pleroma" (fullness) of Chara (Joy)!

- <u>HAVE PROPER SELF CONCEPT</u>: - Your belief system is a major key in creating the world around you. Your life is patterned after your greatest conscious asset or liability in the convolutions of your mind. What you sees, says and believe about yourself is important, and significant in the parlance of wealth creation. You cannot rise above your ultimate concept about yourself.

The Japanese believe in three fundamental dynamics as follows:

a.   The Sword

b.   The Mirror

c.   The Jewel

Note the sword represents military might, the mirror represents self image, or self concept, the jewel represents economic power so their primordial values are built around these frameworks. The Japanese had hoped to become a super world power by the end of the 2nd world war- they built a strong alliance with Adolph Hitler army to fight the war. That hope was crashed by the gallant and brilliance intervention of America and Great Britain. Now, Japan moved away from war to fortify their economy which has grown and advanced vastly in all its ramification, such that, Japan is ahead of America in most technologies that dominates the world market today.

What keeps driving the economy of this Asian Nation is proper self concept. This is quiet reflected in their school system where Japanese language comes first for every student before any foreign language as an elective subject. It is the ability to keep mother tongue that sparks their technology and this is as a result of proper self concept. If you lack proper self concept- you surely lost your own language and your originality. It will take you extra effort to actualize your dreams in life; because you will be building your life with what is outside your originality.

- <u>POLISH YOURSELF IMAGE</u>: - Proper self image is everything to wealth creation. To have a proper self concept that is not capped with a bloated self image is as good as eating all white rice without stew.

Self concept deals with your inner self and its healthiness while self image addresses your outer healthiness and ultimate packaging appearance-wise. It is important you wear your dream on your look every day before it ever materializes. Dress the way you want people to address in the near future. It does not cost fortune to look your best all the time. Take time to re-brand your self-image so that you will be in business for yourself and be in money. God dressing and proper carriage has the magic wand to open all doors of help and businesses for you.

Change your associates if they do not fit into your dream, and do not hesitate to restrict yourself to only place of significant and importance to your dream. You can quit partying around with useless folks on the street to join a golf club or entrepreneur club where you meet the CEOs, principals and financial money bags of your community. Such places enhance your personality and more so, hype your chances to secure a business deal that could launch your dream into reality. Such places celebrate business ventures and lofty financial projects, so good business idea easily gets recognized and receives either outright sponsorship or partnership or even both packages.

Good self image inspires confidence, give you undaunting carriage and make you talk with panache. You may not necessarily have money in your pocket to be in your best mood and best look. When people are meeting you for the first time, their feelers are up in the air like the CNN Masts to gauge your passion, self esteem, and confidence, degree of relaxation in your carriage and level of intelligence that you exude. It is this that opens them up to listen to you, attach importance to your words or ideas, and attach significance to either your products or services. Life coaches or public speakers will continue to rule their world because this concept of self image is the encrypted code behind their business success.

- <u>PROPER SELF IMAGE = VENTURE CAPITAL</u>: - Proper self- image is a venture capital that you need to become a millionaire you desire badly. Dare to cut your hair and give it a person brand to make a statement of a kind. Stand before the mirror to practice good body posture that says "I am significant in my world. Add other body language that speaks volumes into the air whenever you talk or sit to discuss with someone one-on-one or in a group. Practice confident smile before people. it sends the message home that you are a personality of a brand. Personally, I call such smile: "my resource control gesture", it opens the door to every heart for me. You cannot do much in life if you do not have proper self image.

Finally on this note, read good books that can enhances your grammar, diction and improve on your eloquence. Business 95% is all about speaking to people to convince them into partnership tie deals or make them buy your products or services.

- <u>GO BEYOND CREATING PRODUCTS OR SERVICES; CREATE A COMPETITIVE BRAND TO SOAK UP YOUR MARKET NICHE</u>: - The entire globe has moved away from buying just for the utility of a product or service to buying unique names that is branding. Coca cola is a brand, 7up is a brand, Microsoft Corporation amasses billions from their brand, and so others. Ever before you set out to create a product or service- have branding at the back of the mind. Branding is what gives a product or service the original "buzz" in the marketplace. For instance, Facebook is a global brand in social networking industry. It stands out astute with a profound signature in its structural configuration and flexibility in its friendly screen interface.

- <u>THINKING RICH CAN MAKE YOUR STINKING RICH</u>: - Everything begins with thinking and ends with thinking. The ability to think right makes live right, talk right and relate rightly with others. Your first major import in the business arena is good thinking. If you are defeated in the mind you can hardly think victory as a possibility or reality. No matter where you are now in life, you can always go beyond your limitation at the moment only if you can think very well. Everything around you responds to your thought projection, so if you project negative thoughts into people or circumstances around you, surely you get a negative outcome, and vice versa.

Your mind has the capacity to hold things firm and flip them into reality if rightly engaged. The Universe is loaded with much more abundant supply of all things than any wild imagination could fathom. You do not access the cornucopia of wealth of the universe by mere random vibration of encoded ideas in your mind. You have to train your mind to look deep intently and more purposeful to envision yourself in your life dream. This exercise will give you the deep seated serenity you require to build your kind of world where impossibility does not exist. If all barriers are removed from your mind- then start thinking big and you get big outcomes on your way. I will encouraged you to pick a copy of my all time best seller "Wealth Oracle……" to learn more about the dynamics of wealthy thinking. This book has worked out miracles in several lives across the globe. Your life is going to be among the latest wealth big bang miracles across the globe ever before you hit the last chapter of that book. it is a reality in rarity!

Start thinking where you are now, and watch yourself gradually sinking into unlimited supply of waters of riches. You cannot fail in life with catalog of right thinking smeared with concrete referential actions dotting every jot of your mind. Thinking rich can make you stinking rich and make you stay rich for life.

- <u>CUT OUT YOUR FINANCIAL DREAMS ON A SOLID BRICK</u>: - You don't get far in life or in anything useful without a definite goal. No matter the magnitude of your financial dream- You will only step into it if you have them well spelt out on a concrete brick of actions. That is solid financial plan or goal.

Ritchie Felix,
Copyright by Ritchie Felix

You have to know how much money you want in life that will be enough for your dream life style- that is your financial target. Break this compact figures into per annum and then into months. This makes your dream attainable, measurable and specific to the letter. Then, began to allot date you will make your first money, and then move to the rest.

This way you become SMART in your approach to financial issues, especially your financial goal.

The Word "SMART" is in acronym as

S = Specific, A = attainable, R = reliable, T = time lag. Your financial goal must circumvent within this SMART circumference. It is also you take into cognizance your "SWORT" to really become financial literate at the end of the day, and stay rich all your life.

Again, the word: "SWOT" is in acronym as

S = Strength, you have to know your highest strength in terms of ability and capacity for productivity

W = Weakness, you have to know the oddities that will clog your possible progress. Identify your financial weakness in terms of attitude and usage of money, and take care of it so that your dream can become a reality

O = Opportunity, take inventory of all the opportunities opening up around the corner nationally and globally, even start with the ones in your neighborhood first. There abound opportunities in every challenge, find it out and explore it to your advantage

T = Threats, find out the possible threats that can stop you or thwart your effort in both short and long terms. Look for alternative ways to overcome it or get a plan B as a back up for your financial goal. No matter the threats around, know this for sure, there is always a trail to every threat. So, locate this trail and use it to find the root of the threat or way out of it.

THE FOUR THINGS TO NOTE ABOUT GOALS

- Know where you are going from where you are at the moment
- Discover what it takes to get there
- Discover who and what is connected to your goal
- Give it all it takes

• ## TEN FUNDAMENTAL UNIVERSAL LAWS OF GOAL SETTING:-

1. Goals must be achievable

2. Goals must have time duration or lag

3. Goals must be specific in both short run and long run.

4. Goals must be set base on the target in focus and not base on the realities on ground at the moment or instance of dream

5. Goals must engage your energy and synergy of partners

6. Goals must be attainable

7. Goals must be reliable

8. Goals must be broken down into smaller units of actions in a logical sequential order.

9. Goals must be object of your ambition, vision and direction

10. Goals must be measurable at any given time.

Note, until you set out your financial goals- you are still far from stepping into unlimited supply of money. No matter how clear your dream is, cut it out on a financial bricks of action to stay on course.

- GO BEYOND FINANCIAL INTELLIGENCE, GROW YOUR MARKET INTELLIGENCE:- Financial literacy is not taught in our schools but a direct import of financial intelligence, same way market intelligence produces market literacy. Market intelligence involves actual analysis of consumers behaviour in respect to product to service value at a given price mechanism per time, and what the consumers spends their money and how often. This is more of practical than mere theoretical exegesis devoid of exactitudes of empirical practices. The end point is usually market intelligence which arms the business man with the right info to base his targeted production or services offer.

Market intelligence creates the platform and give you the

bearings to control the market with the antics & tool you have developed in the course of your market literacy. Growing in your mastery of the market enables you encode hidden business existing around known business that is not known or known but not yet explored. The followings point out in none-material terms what market intelligence is all about.

- Market intelligence is the conscious ability to know what people spends their money on, how often they spend it.

- It knows what problem an invention or innovation will

solve, how will it add or meet needs or reduce the societal challenge(s) and make life more comfortable.

► Market intelligence involves knowing what vacuum in the human society life an idea or product or service can fill.

► It knows how variety can conveniently replace monotony or break down monopoly.

► Market intelligence is the ability to know what obtains in the future market with the correlation of the reality on ground at the moment.

- It is the reasoning that tries to plot in real terms the performance peak of the market in the near future for any given item, creativity, fashion, technology and services. It is the bridge that links the future from where you are to give the strategic positioning in the market to scoop great advantage as realty unfolds in the market places.

- Market intelligence finds out what challenges exist in the society or in a given commodity or service market, and what type or degree of solutions is required, how can these solutions be packaged and what model of distribution channel should be deployed. Again, at what quantity or quality or price tag it will be sold. What parameters should be engaged to evaluate the utility of such product or service or what satisfaction will the final consumers derive from it.

Furthermore, market intelligence is the direct result of market fore-sight base on several definite indicators with respect to consumerism or consumer's behavior or reaction specific product or service category either existing or new in the market. Having the proper market intelligence about the business axis you intend to enter, give you the advantage to know the type of capital you require to start and what volume, and the exact where to start.

In the Information Age, money is very important to all and sundry same way information is essential to the growth of a business. Having strong market intelligence enables you to process every information to personal knowledge in order to intersect the volume of money in circulation with the right tool kits of financial intelligence.

You should be able to know where money is flowing to and why, and how. Financial intelligence utilizes the outcome of market intelligence to decipher from which product or service market that money is flowing from why and how. This is always accessible from the information in the thin air.

CHAPTER FIVE

TWELVE WAYS TO RAISE CAPITAL FOR YOUR BUSINESS IDEA OR VISION

Dreaming big is not enough or having a lofty vision alone do not guarantee success or bring reward of any sort: it is the actual execution of your dream or business idea that create cash flow and success from the void. Several people with great dreams, visions or business ideas never go beyond the grail walls of dreaming to establishing it in reality because the lack capital for a start. Like I said earlier, that what you need to be in business is either money capital or venture capital (i.e. an idea or confidence/poise). In most cases, it is obvious you need to start with money. This chapter will tell you how, checks below the follow twelve ways or places to raise capital for your business idea or vision.

- <u>FRIENDS & ASSOCIATES</u>: - You can approach well meaning friends or associates to share your business ideas or dreams with the mind to secure financial assistance to key into your vision. Often, this traditional method has been major means to secure either primary or secondary capital for a start. But, you have to be very smart in both

Ritchie Felix,
Copyright by Ritchie Felix

the area of sharing this business idea and getting the individual convinces to open his wallet for you. In sharing the idea, you are not under compulsion to highlight so much on the strong points of your business idea in order not to expose much so that such will not be stolen from you. This information Age, another hearing from you the details of your business idea with all its nitty-gritty can develop the idea ahead of you and be in the market place before your actual arrival. this will break up the monopoly you would have enjoyed in that business. So beware who to share your dream or business idea with.

- <u>INTERNET CASH ECONOMY</u>: - The Internet is the best place to raise either primary or secondary capital for your business. There is over $3.38 Trillion flowing through the internet daily, and you can divert good sum of this cash flow into your personal pocket. How is this possible? Use the search engines to locate blog directories, sign up for blogging in sites like word press, blogger.com, kontera, Hubpage.com and others, then, configure Google Adsense to your blogs, and in just few months you flood your bank account with money. It is that easy and requires no money for a start. All you need here is write up good articles garnished with profitable keywords to optimize the search engines. And as visitors click on the Google adverts on your site or blog your wallet clicks with cash flow. There are also several other ways to raise money from the internet cash economy. If you are a novice in this area contact me via my email for assistance or take up personal training courses or coaching session in this area.

- <u>INTELLECTUAL PROPERTY</u>:- You can raise good cash from an own intellectual properties like website, blogs, graphic designs, books, music, copyrighted materials, trademarks, picture, idea, etc. In the information age, your motion picture is an intellectual property that can be sold over and over again to several sites at ebay.com including amazon.com. Such picture usually depicts concepts that serve as web theme or template use by webmasters.

More so, you can package your childhood experiences as

storybook for children that you can submit to free sites or register it to secure the copyright and create loads of cash flow from it. Again if you are novice here- you contact me or take up courses in that area either online or offline.

- <u>PARTNERSHIP</u>: - Share your business idea with a willing friend or associate who can decide to come into the business to share both profit and risk with you either as an active or sleeping or dormant partner. This is how many big businesses started from foundation. Yahoo, Apple Computers, Microsoft

Corporation, and host of others started from this spring board-partnership. In most cases, this is the best way to finance your business idea or dream and at the same time give it credibility and the right speed to survive in a competitive environment. Your prospective partner might bring in both money and fundamental skill for a proper take off. Give this a trial. But however, seek the advice of a consultant before trading on this path to understand its dynamics and mechanics as well as its possible demerits.

- <u>PERSONAL SAVINGS</u>: - Many a times, it is difficult to raise money for a start from those around you or those outside your neighborhood. This does not mean that, your idea or dream is on the negative or that they do not believe in you- it may be sheer fate playing prangs on you. Don not shelve your business idea to a corner, rather devise a way to money in trickles to culminate to lump some, then, you start off with it. Some people you met before now might show up later when the business is already ticking with life. But it is very important you do not kill your dream by dumping to fate for lack of capital.

Michael Dell saved money to register his Dell Computers corporation in 1984. It was an uncommon feat that saw him rose through the woods of challenges to dominate the PCs market ahead of IBM. Today, his PCs sales across the globe. In his book, Direct from Dell: Strategies that Revolutionized an Industry, Michael told his story. He said that one day his parents paid him a surprise visit. His father was disappointed by the distraction hls son was enmcshed in his dormitory. The old man snapped

"Get your priorities straight: What do you want to do with your life?". But the young Michael replied boldly: "I want to compete with IBM!" The parents never supported with a capital for a start, but he started. You can start with what is in your hand now no matter where you are. You are the only person who understand your dream, who can interpret the impulses in your nervous system and who can actually give life to your dream or business idea. Save money and start off!

You can sell off shoes, electronics, and personal assets to

raise money for your business. It saves you much headache to start with your own money.

- <u>MULTILEVEL MARKETING BUSINESS</u>: - There are so many MLMs out there on the streets. Take time to research them out, and join one with good profiteering scheme and training programs. This will help you raise enough money for a take off with your business idea, and on the long run you can leverage on this platform to even expand the scope of your business. Any good MLM pays with definite and infinite money. You earn and learn at same time giving yourself the ultimate lifestyle in life. It is the **learning** aspect that pays with infinite money because you can leverage on the teachings at workshops and public campaigns

- <u>FUND RAISING</u>: - You can organize a fundraising meeting in your neighborhood or in your church to raise money for your business. This is easy if you can get an influential adult person who can support your dream. Or you can liaise with your church Minister to use his good Ecclesiastical position to raise financial supporters to sponsor your business idea or vision. Several celebrities in the music industry started off their career from the church they attended. You can remember vividly the fundraising exercise that swept across the globe to support President Barrack Obama during his presidential campaign. The man brandish a nice script for his campaign, the support in monetary term came unsolicited. With a clear cut script describing your business mission, goals, objectives, and as well a snapshot of estimated income in view, people will want to idcntify with your vision.

- <u>TRADE YOUR TALENTS AND GIFTS</u>:- In Nigeria, in the west Africa of Sub-Sahara region- several young people have discovered raw talents in sports like football, table tennis, boxing, swimming, writing, music and others as major sources to raise money to start out in life. This a time goes with skill building to cash on certain opportunities around. Every individual on earth has talents, gifts or skills that can be converted to cash if adequately and properly engaged. You can raise capital for a business idea using your talents or gifts. I started out very early in life to use my speaking skill to raise money for my studies while in the university. I featured severally in many events as M.C, Guest speaker, resource people in workshops, instructor, teaching and public campaigns in various youth groups or organization did work with. I raised quiet huge amount through this simple hobby which today have translated into a global career as life coach/consultant and all that.

- USE "OPT" AND "OPM":- Dream or vision that is sustainable over time usually involves others directly or indirectly. It is expedient that you do not allow fear, superiority complex or egocentrism to stop you from engaging the free help around you or your corner to cash on your dream. "OPT" – other people talent and "OPM"- other people money are two extremes that must surely interplay I your vision actualization. Endeavour to tap into these available resources to make a start.

Take time to look deep within your domain to take stock of available talents of people that are relevant to your vision. Again, do not hesitate to ask for financial assistance from senior friends or even mate that can assist you for a start. These way money self-made millionaires cashed on the dreams and roll in money.

- <u>SELL OTHER PEOPLE STUFF</u>: - Selling is the heart beat of 21st century commerce across the world axes. You do need money to start selling other people stuffs. In most cases, you do not need to be a regular staff of a firm or company to sell their products or services. For instance, you can go online to sign up affiliate packages with ebay.com, amazon.com and click bank. After signing up, you get your affiliate links with which you can sell their products and track your performance with ease. Several people have started out this way, and today they are big timers in the society.

Around your neighborhood, check to find out those who want to sell their old stuffs, then, you can contract this business, and start making money immediately. Save some to build up your capital for your proposed business venture.

• <u>DO REAL ESTATE AGENT BUSINESS</u>: - Ordinarily, you do need money to do this business in most parts of the world. You can decide to partner with others who are legally registered and have license in this business. Share your intention with your choice estate agent and begin to secure deals that can be followed up gradually until it is put through. Normally, any deal secured through, you earn a commission base upon the agreed sharing formula or percentage. In the long-run, you will build up enough equity base or capital to start off on your primary business.

- <u>SELL AN OWN STUFF</u>: - This is one of the easiest ways to raise quick money to start off a business idea. You can sell clothes, gold coin, silver plague, artifacts and even used shores. There are severally markets online or offline where such capital derivatives can be converted into money.

  Also, if you have written a book before, you can decide to sell of the original manuscripts of ebay.com or at Amazon. The original manuscripts of best selling books are usually purchase by either government or private enterprise can decide to buy it for keeps in the museum to raise money in the near future. You can even sell an own pictures to several sites online while serves as great tool for the webmasters in theme and site template design respectively.

Just look enough to see what you have that can convert into watering lump sum, then, go into cool business for yourself. Be in pool of money.

Chapter Six
Be In Business for Yourself

"Basic element of business in Knowledge age"

In the world of business in the present global knowledge economy; it is important to arm yourself up to the teeth to make it any business. Below are the basic elements of business you must know to be thick in success as follows:

➢ **YOU:** You are the fundamental asset of the business. The most integral parts of every function or operation revolve around your business prowess. Your personal qualities either good or bad can make or mar your business. It is important that you have the following good qualities to make your business thick as follows: Honesty, tolerance, presentable, resourceful, creativity, considerate, enthusiasm, hardworking and cheerfulness.

Also, note the following bad qualities will destroy your business as follows: dishonesty, selfishness, laziness, unreliable, pessimistic, fraudulent, extravagant, carelessness, nonchalant, etc.

Good qualities solidify the foundation of your business in the wisdom age while bad quality places a limitation on your business growth and relationship.

➢ **THE CUSTOMER:** The customer is the king in the market place, and he is always right. In the market spaces on the web the customer is referred to as traffic. To succeed in business in the wisdom age, you have to know the following about customers:

(a) What group of people are your potential customers?

(b) How to focus your products and services to meet their needs

(c) Customers buy what they need, and only few buy because of your sales pitch.

(d) Customer is a king and always right or you lost him to your close competition in the market

(e) Your marketing antics can attract new customers and keep old ones

Note, if you must build loyal customers and take your business to the next glorious level- you have to be professional, be punctual, be consistent in quality of your product or service, keep promises, automate your business system and keep learning new things daily.

Nevertheless, the customers consider the following factors to make a request:-

= Product or service quality

= supplier reputation

= Product or service price

= prompt delivery

= quick response to customer's need

= Product/service testimonials

= Shipment rate competitiveness

= service innovativeness

= Product/service competitive edge over other close substitutes in the market, etc.

➢ **THE PRODUCT/SERVICE: -** In the present global knowledge economy, the entire world has shrunk into a neighborhood on the golden platform of the internet. There is much more competition in the market place than before. You have to target your product/service to meet the needs of a particular community or niche. You have to leverage your marketing style from product or service marketing to audience marketing. It is important you emphasize more on what your audience will benefit from your product/service, and less emphasize on the loads of advantages of your product/services.

- **FINANCE:** - It is smart business practice to open and run a current account in your company's name. This will help you to access bank facilities and secure travel documents to seek for either distributors or suppliers abroad. You are in business to maximize profits and so you have to develop good financial ethic to protect your hard earned money. You do not have keep cash around you to avoid temptation to spend it on impulse buy. The finance is the blood or life-wire of any business after idea.

More so, keep good record of your accounting system using pager and autopilot among many others. Have a database of your loyal customers as they represent both your market share and profit quotient in business. It is important you discover and develop a good financial credit facility for your customers to give them sense of belonging in your business. This usually results to long term customer loyalty even in the face of adverse competition. Customers tend to stick to the business that grants credit leverage. You must be wise enough to keep such credit facility soft and sure so, that on the long run the business will not hit shipwreck.

♦ **SKILL: -** Useful business skill is anything to business from North to South and from East to West, just same way air is to any living thing around. Skill can be learnt, discovered, developed and deployed to work out wonders. You have to take conscious inventory of your business skill before you set out to start up one. Having knowledge of this basic requirement positions you to either employ yourself solely or engage others to achieve your goal in business. You may not be lucky to have all the skills that will make your business thick with success and tinker high and higher in growth. Then, you must engage an expert to recruit for you the right skillful personnel to work with. This might you a little mite and pays you back in many beautiful ways.

♦   So many people who are in business today and are making it high in profits have the surefire skills that drive the axle of the business. It is not just the location of their business that is the fundamental   element   in determining their profit; rather it is their uncommon skill at work. On the other hand, lack of useful and relevant business skill can ground your business and plunge you into bankruptcy.

CAPITAL: Capital can be money or its prototype in the form of idea, expertise or formula. You do not have to wait for ages to get paper currency before setting out to start your business. You can start with whatever thing you have at hand no matter how small or insignificant just makes attempt to start up something where you are now. Every average business man you see around started small before growing the business into something big.

GOD:- God runs the biggest industry on earth and has all the formulae to business success. He is into the business of creating human beings, and managing the entire activities of His creatures on earth. Aligning your thoughts and creative ideas with Divine-supreme intelligence give you the right footage and bearing to see your way to superlative success. If you have these fundamental elements in place, then, you are on your way to record outstanding success.

HOW TO IDENTIFY A MARKETIBLE BUSINESS IDEA

New talent combines effectively, efficiently and timely with useful and relevant skill it forms a viable business idea. Every individual is gifted by Mother Nature to the degree that can culminate into ultimate ends, means and satisfaction in life. It is important you know this from albinitio that you are an integral part of your business. Your personality, skills, talent and resources will play essential role in developing a business idea that will work for you and make you be in business.

Every society or community has its needs and there always exist in such environment-various levels of socio-economic strata with special needs. Changes in taste of fashion with respect to rapidly changing socio-economic structure and the demand for development and globalization all inter-play to alter the nature and level of need for members of these classes. At this, there is necessity to search and continue to search out ways and better ways to identify an appropriate market idea that deliver adequately the demands for value of the evoking needs of various levels of classes in the society. You need to follow the steps below to identify marketable business idea:

♦ **Develop a Marketable idea**: - To be able to come up with something that will worth a headache, you need to know what exactly the need of your potential customers is. You should be able to tell who they are and their location. Find a way to gauge the quantity of their demand in advance, and from this- you can identify a parameter to ensure a repeat purchase. Then, a good and suitable business idea will peculate fro the void naturally upon your mind.

♦ **Look at Your skills**: - You need to take inventory of your skills that are relevant to actualize your business idea. There may be needed to go for inquiry from an expert or consultant in that area of business venture. Any way, you can lone your skills to upgrade it to fit into your business idea template. On the other hand, you may need to engage temporally or permanently someone that has the right skill. It is advisable you either go for skill acquisition program in the direction of your business idea or engage someone temporally for a start.

Then, gradually understudy him/her, and before long show the back door.

♦ **Discover, develop & deploy your talent**: Your talent is the natural abilities endowed in you from birth. Find your talent that is in line with your business idea and develop it so that you can optimize profit in the long run. It is advisable your business idea should evolve around your talent so that you do not struggle to get desired results.

Being in business is not about luck; it is about applying tested and proven principles to whatever you do; principles that have been around for many years works irrespective of "who" and "where" and "when" it was applied. The law of gravity is universal-same way most business principles works. Throw anything up under the earth in the night or day, in Africa or in Asia, it surely comes down to the earth under the influence of acceleration due to gravity. Identify the right and profitable business idea and be in business of money.

••
••••••••••••••••••••••••••••••••

You must be in business for yourself. You must have own

product/service in the present global economy to give up to another for valuable exchange for money. It is most profitable if you parade an own wares before the world, and write up your scripts to roll in super-abundant money. This is only a possibility if you dare to identify a marketable business idea that works on regular basis. This article will take you further to shield light on the following steps to take help you be in business:

♦ **Look at your resources**: Resources here includes tangible and intangible assets that can serve as standard of value or exchange to enable you start up a business in earnest. It is wise you see money, skills, friends, contacts, talent, and creativity as resources. Take inventory of your own stock of resources and this will subsequently inform your choice of business, approach and strategy for your business operation.

Owning a profitable business or businesses not run by you is a source of real income. As the globe shrinks rapidly, it is more advisable you identify business idea that can run independently to enable you have time to maximizes your leisure. Having competent team players at the helm of your business affairs is real resource and invaluable assets to your business. When you set up a business that is successfully managed by others independent of your presence, then you are surely on your way to financial independent.

Huge profits that keep rolling in on regular basis-whether you are there or not is one of the fundamental reason that make you bc in business. It is the ultimate expectation of every business guru. If you study the most successful people across the globe, and they have simply done this better than anyone else and made large amount of money profit in the process. You can create your own success story if you dare work on your marketable business idea.

♦ **Look at for business in same arena of your idea to link up with**: - It is a common mistake people made in the era of industrialization to "re-invent" the wheel in setting up new business venture. You can link up with an existing business in that area of your business idea to share support and resources with each other. It is a sound business secret to be innovative in order to enjoy that competitive edge over other existing businesses.

RULES TO MAXIMIZE YOUR Profitable BUSINESS IDEA

1. Do not set up a business until you have clear cut vision framed around on definite purpose

2. Do not start a business you do not possess the basic skill or talent to operate

3. Do not enter into a business with a mindset of trial and error. Be in business for the real mission of your life.

4. Do not enter into a business base on other people experience and conviction.

5. Do not enter into a business if its market niche is already saturated.

Finally, the unvarnished truth so far is that, you must gain priceless insight into what your market audience really need and want to be very successful and be in money.

"3 WAYS PEOPLE DEVELOP FINANCIAL LIMITATION IN THE WISDOM AGE"

The mission of this article is to flaunt to the bare eyes walls of limitation people have created over their finances for ages based on erroneous beliefs unorthodox practices and for lack of financial intelligence. If you know this and avoid it, then, you ride on the wings of success and roll your self in money.

1. **Verbal Programming: -** This is constituted of all that you "HEARD" when you were young and passing through various schools of life. What did you hear about money, wealth and rich people when you were growing up? Did you ever hear thing like?

- Save money for the rainy day
- Rich people are greedy
- Money comes at God's time

- Money does not grown on trees
- Big certificate, big job and fat salary
- The rich get richer, the poor get poorer
- Money is the root of all evil
- No formal education, no money or financial security
- Money is made for adult minds
- Money brings unhappiness and anxiety leading to hypertension
- That is not for people like us
- Background determines front ground
- You do not work hard for money, if your father did not pass on wealth to you.

- the list continue to count

These infamous statements as listed above, that you have heard over time have gradually but surely sink deep into the grail matter of your mind sub-consciousness and are running your financial life. You have to conscious unlearned yourself of negative issues of this degradable status to reclaim back your financial life.

2. **Modeling:-** The second day people develop financial limitation is called modeling. This is the bane of poverty in many lives and homes today from Africa to Asia, USA to

Europe and from Caribbean to Australia. People usually toe same financial line or belief system of their parents or any authority figure over their life in their childhood. If you can answer the following questions below sincerely, you surely discover a way out of your limitations as follows:

▶ What were your parents or guardian like in the arena of money when you were growing up?

▶ Did one or both of them managed their funds well or did they turned them over to others/reports to manage for them?

▶ Were they spenders or savers?

- Did they have enough financial education to achieve financial freedom?

- Were they non-investors or shrewd investors?

- Did one or both worked hard to earn money or did they put money to work hard for them?

- Was money the source of joy in your house or point of argument?

It is important to take cognizance of all the above listed as negative childhood experience has a way to replay itself in your adulthood life. If you are still pre-conditioned with these negatives there is no way you can make a headway out of financial mess.

3. **Specific Incidents:** - What you experience while still growing up somehow account for about 86% of your belief system. What did you experience concerning money, wealth, and rich people while you were young? These experiences are shaping your concept and belief system of money. Little wonder, you are facing difficulties financially at present you can trace way back to where you started in life.

    Belief system can be learned and there force can be unlearned. You do this by switching off from the negative and switching on to the positive.

UNEMPLOYED- HOW YOU CAN BEAT THE PANGS OF ECONOMIC CHALLENGES

The number of people unemployed in 2008 in just four countries rolls as shown below:

China-   6.7Million

Japan-   2,650.000

Spain-   2, 590,000

USA-   8, 924,000

As 2009 began, the world looked up to newly elected USA President, Barrack Obama, for a possible salvation from the claws of financial crisis and near zero employment of the masses. In the 1980s, government bailouts were in the millions. By the 1990s, they were in billions. And today, as more people lost their precious jobs to imminent financial turmoil, they are in the trillions. Yet, the jobs are hard to come by as things get worse by every minute of the day. Many jobs have gone abroad, and companies are wobbling on their feet in fear of glaring onset of great depression around the corner.

Loss of a job or unemployment creates more than financial strain. Often it cuts to the very core of your grail matter. If you are out of job and stay for too long without getting another; you begin to lose confidence in yourself and that air of importance around your person sublime into the air. People treat you as nothing, and before long you begin to view yourself the way they view you.

As if the emotional trauma that comes with long unemployment were not enough, each person who joins the rank of the unemployed faces the additional challenges of living on less. It is against this background that I write this article to help you beat the pangs of anxiety, mental rot and financial crisis of the imminent recession, with the following impeccable antidotes:

- ♦ **Shop Wisely;-** Plan your weekly menu around what is on sale that are in your favor. Buy basic condiments instead of pre-packaged food items, and cook from scratch. Take time to stock up seasonal items as they are cheap during the season. Purchase in bulk, but be careful not to overstock perishable items. Slash down on clothing costs by opting rather for second hand clothes at the resale stores. Now you are unemployed, make out time to locate the nearest resale store in your neighborhood. Cut back on how often you shop, especially, if you are the one winning he bread for the family at the moment to keep your marriage and home together.

♦ **Be resourceful, creative and innovative:**- It is important you cut down on non-essentials, find out the liabilities around you to trade for money. Things like used car, used books, used clothes and children toys that are still in better condition to be use by a second party. Even be more resourceful to do the followings:-

-    Plant a garden and grow your own vegetables

Ritchie Felix,
Copyright by Ritchie Felix

- Use your good clothing on special occasion
- Switch off gas and the power system when going out or not in use to save money for other things.
- Cut down on habitual spending spree
- Avoid cinema occasionally, it is more advisable to eliminate about 2 to 3 habits in your life at the moment to get better in your finances
- Spend less to entertain friends and business associates

- Develop new set of money-making skills or turn hobbies into money-making activity.
- Boycott a meal to save money for tomorrow or other things.

If you can diligently practice all that is enumerated so far in this article, sure – you beat the pangs of unemployment or what do you think?

CHAPTER SEVEN

TWELVE WAYS TO RAISE CAPITAL FOR YOUR BUSINESS IDEA OR VISION

Dreaming big is not enough or having a lofty vision alone do not guarantee success or bring reward of any sort: it is the actual execution of your dream or business idea that create cash flow and success from the void. Several people with great dreams, visions or business ideas never go beyond the grail walls of dreaming to establishing it in reality because the lack capital for a start. Like I said earlier, that what you need to be in business is either money capital or venture capital (i.e. an idea or confidence/poise). In most cases, it is obvious you need to start with money. This chapter will tell you how, checks below the follow twelve ways or places to raise capital for your business idea or vision.

- FRIENDS & ASSOCIATES: - You can approach well meaning friends or associates to share your business ideas or dreams with the mind to secure financial assistance to key into your vision. Often, this traditional method has been major means to secure either primary or secondary capital for a start. But, you have to be very smart in both the area of sharing this business idea and getting the individual convince to open his wallet for you. In sharing the idea, you are not under compulsion to highlight so much on the strong points of your business idea in order not to expose much so that such will not be stolen from you. This information Age, another hearing from you the details of your business idea with all its nitty-gritty can develop the idea ahead of you and be in the market place before your actual arrival. this will break up the monopoly you would have enjoyed in that business. So beware who to share your dream or business idea with.

- INTERNET CASH ECONOMY:- The Internet is the best place to raise either primary or secondary capital for your business. There is over $3.38 Trillion flowing through the internet daily, and you can divert good sum of this cash flow into your personal pocket. How is this possible? Use the search engines to locate blog directories, sign up for blogging in sites like wordpress, blogger.com, kontera, Hubpage.com and others, then, configure Google Adsense to your

Ritchie Felix,
Copyright by Ritchie Felix

blogs, and in just few months you flood your bank account with money. It is that easy and require no money for a start. All you need here is write up good articles garnished with profitable keywords to optimize the search engines. And as visitors click on the Google adverts on your site or blog your wallet clicks with cash flow. There are also several other ways to raise money from the internet cash economy. If you are a novice in this area contact me via my email for assistance or take up personal training courses or coaching session in this area.

- INTELLECTUAL PROPERTY:- You can raise good cash from an own intellectual properties like website, blogs, graphic designs, books, music, copyrighted materials, trademarks, picture, idea, etc. In the information age, your motion picture is an intellectual property that can be sold over and over again to several sites at ebay.com including amazon.com. Such picture usually depicts concepts that serve as web theme or template use by webmasters.

More so, you can package your childhood experiences as

storybook for children that you can submit to free sites or register it to secure the copyright and create loads of cash flow from it. Again if you are novice here- you contact me or take up courses in that area either online or offline.

- PARTNERSHIP:- Share your business idea with a willing friend or associate who can decide to come into the business to share both profit and risk with you either as an active or sleeping or dormant partner. This is how many big businesses started from foundation. Yahoo, Apple Computers, Microsoft

Corporation, and host of others started from this spring board-partnership. In most cases, this is the best way to finance your business idea or dream and at the same time give it credibility and the right speed to survive in a competitive environment. Your prospective partner might bring in both money and fundamental skill for a proper take off. Give this a trial. But however, seek the advice of a consultant before trading on this path to understand its dynamics and mechanics as well as its possible demerits.

- PERSONAL SAVINGS:- Many atimes, it is difficult to raise money for a start from those around you or those outside your neighborhood. This do not mean that, your idea or dream is on the negative or that they do not believe in you- it may be sheer fate playing prangs on you. Don not sholve your business idea to a corner, rather devise a way to money in trickles to culminate to lumpsome, then, you start off with it. Some people you met before now might show up later when the business is already ticking with life. But it is very important you do not kill your dream by dumping to fate for lack of capital.

Michael Dell saved money to register his Dell Computers corporation in 1984. It was an uncommon feat that saw him rose through the woods of challenges to dominate the PCs market ahead of IBM. Today, his PCs sales across the globe. In his book, Direct from Dell: Strategies that Revolutionized an Industry, Michael told his story. He said that one day his parents paid him a surprise visit. His father was disappointed by the distraction his son was enmeshed in his dormitory. The old man snapped

"Get your priorities straight: What do you want to do with your life?". But the young Michael replied boldly: "I want to compete with IBM!" The parents never supported with a capital for a start, but he started. You can start with what is in your hand now no matter where you are. You are the only person who understand your dream, who can interpret the impulses in your nervous system and who can actually give life to your dream or business idea. Save money and start off!

You can sell off shoes, electronics, and personal assets to

raise money for your business. It saves you much headache to start with your own money.

- MULTILEVEL MARKETING BUSINESS:- There are so many MLMs out there on the streets. Take time to research them out, and join one with good profiteering scheme and training programs. This will help you raise enough money for a take off with your business idea, and on the long run you can leverage on this platform to even expand the scope of your business. Any good MLM pays with definite and infinite money. You earn and learn at same time giving yourself the ultimate lifestyle in life. It is the **learning** aspect that pays with infinite money because you can leverage on the teachings at workshops and public campaigns

- FUND RAISING:- You can organize a fundraising meeting in your neighborhood or in your church to raise money for your business. This is easy if you can get an influential adult person who can support your dream. Or you can liase with your church Minister to use his good Ecclesiastical position to raise financial supporters to sponsor your business idea or vision. Several celebrities in the music industry started off their career from the church they attended. You can remember vividly the fundraising exercise that swept across the globe to support President Barrack Obama during his presidential campaign. The man brandish a nice script for his campaign, the support in monetary term came unsolicited. With a clear cut script describing your business mission, goals, objectives, and as well a snapshot of estimated income inview, people will want to identify with your vision.

- TRADE YOUR TALENTS AND GIFTS:- In Nigeria, in the west Africa of Sub-Sahara region- several young people have discovered raw talents in sports like football, table tennis, boxing, swimming, writing, music and others as major sources to raise money to start out in life. This atimes goes with skill building to cash on certain opportunities around. Every individual on earth has talents, gifts or skills that can be converted to cash if adequately and properly engaged. You can raise capital for a business idea using your talents or gifts. I started out very early in life to use my speaking skill to raise money for my studies while in the university. I featured severally in many events as M.C, Guest speaker, resource people in workshops, instructor, teaching and public campaigns in various youth groups or organization did work with. I raised quiet huge amount through this simple hobby which today have translated into a global career as life coach/consultant and all that.

- USE "OPT" AND "OPM":- Dream or vision that is sustainable over time usually involves others directly or indirectly. It is expedient that you do not allow fear, superiority complex or egocentrism to stop you from engaging the free help around you or your corner to cash on your dream. "OPT" – other people talent and "OPM"- other people money are two extremes that must surely interplay I your vision actualization. Endeavour to tap into these available resources to make a start.

Take time to look deep within your domain to take stock of available talents of people that are relevant to your vision. Again, do not hesitate to ask for financial assistance from senior friends or even mate that can assist you for a start. These way money self-made millionaires cashed on the dreams and roll in money.

- SELL OTHER PEOPLE STUFF:- Selling is the heart beat of 21st century commerce across the world axes. You do need money to start selling other people stuffs. In most cases, you do not need to be a regular staff of a firm or company to sell their products or services. For instance, you can go online to sign up affiliate packages with ebay.com, amazon.com and click bank. After signing up, you get your affiliate links with which you can sell their products and track your performance with ease. Several people have started out this way, and today they are big timers in the society.

Around your neighborhood, check to find out those who want to sell their old stuffs, then, you can contract this business, and start making money immediately. Save some to build up your capital for your proposed business venture.

- DO REAL ESTATE AGENT BUSINESS:- Ordinarily, you do need money to do this business in most parts of the world. You can decide to partner with others who are legally registered and have license in this business. Share your intention with your choiced estate agent and begin to secure deals that can be followed up gradually until it is put through. Normally, any deal secured through, you earn a commission base upon the agreed sharing formula or percentage. In the long-run, you will build up enough equity base or capital to start off on your primary business.

- SELL AN OWN STUFF:- This is one of the easiest way to raise quick money to start off a business idea. You can sell clothes, gold coin, silver plague, artifacts and even used shores. There are severally markets online or offline where such capital derivatives can be converted into money.

Also, if you have written a book before, you can decide to sell of the original manuscripts of ebay.com or at amazon. The original manuscripts of best selling books are usually purchase by either government or private enterprise can decide to buy it for keeps in the museum to raise money in the near future. You can even sell an own pictures to several sites online while serves as great tool for the webmasters in theme and site template design respectively.

Just look enough to see what you have that can convert into watering lumpsum, then, going into cool business for yourself. Be in pool of money.

"HOW TO ROB A BANK IN THE KNOWLEDGE AGE WITHOUT A MASK ...... USE DEBTS"

Naturally, the school system trained us to avoid risk, debts, problems and challenges no matter its insignificance. At all time we are bustling to offset debts, mortgage and credit and bills, rentage, overdraft and car loan. Little wonder, with all our effort to live without debt we keep finding ourselves crammed up in worst cases of indebtedness. The answer to this puzzle or paradox is that the currency in your pocket and in your bank account is not money but DEBT in capital letter.

As long as the Federal Reserve, Citi-groups and Central Banks of the world keep creating money from the thin air in the form of derivatives of several sorts, every bill in your pocket and in the bank account keep degenerating in value to its invest ebb- ie Debt. To grow riches under this double standard, the rich people of the world keep robbing banks without mask using the leverage of debts. You too can do same by following this simple advice:

- **Use Debt to finance your business: -** What do you think the rich people in the land do to avoid heavy tax cut? They built systems or business or businesses to create works for the masses fro the money they borrowed from the banks. The legal framework of the society shields them from paying heavy tax while charging much on the income tax. That is to say, while the company you work for pay relatively nothing in taxation, you are saddle with the responsibility of paying much more from your little income. This is blank robbery, but it is done from the inside of the banks. You too can start up your own business.

The banks do not celebrate savers but borrowers who can return them good percentage interest from returns on their investments in business. The Federal Legal framework at all levels celebrate those who create jobs for the society, and that is exactly what the rich folks leverages on to enmesh their hands in cornucopia of wealth of the universe

- **Use Debt to finance your Real Estate business:-** The advent of innovation in medical science has made it possible for the earth to bulge with great population of people. Real estate is a lucrative business that requires large capital outlay for a start. The real estate business provides economic homes for the average people in the society, and also provides magnificent condo for the big boys of the society. It is really a great business.

You do not need to save money to start, rather borrow from the bank to finance your real estate business. But before you go solo to venture into the business it is wise you study the dynamics and mechanics of the system. Having the knowledge when to tie a deal, how to tie a deal and where to secure a deal is great advantage to fast-tracking your profit in the business. Rich people of the world guide this noble secret to get rich and richer.

The Legal Framework of the society also shields you from paying much as tax since you are even helping the government on the long run to provide shelter for the masses. There are many other ways you can employ to rob banks across the world without a mask on your face. I therefore call on you today to spring into action to launch your first business and be in money leveraging on the matrix of the banks derivatives.

TEN DIFFERENCES BETWEEN RICH MIND AND POOR MIND IN THE WISDOM AGE

A poor man is an orphan and has no friends or associates, and a rich man is a son of many fathers and uncles, and friend of many associates from far and wide across the globe. A rich man is a welcome citizen of any Nation on earth, and a poor man is always denied visa to access the breadth and length of the universe. Poverty is contagious like epidemic disease. Poverty is a deadly disease, wealth is the cure.

Riches start from the mind likewise poverty. A rich mind will produce a rich man, while a poor mind will produce a poor man. Therefore get the ten differences between rich mind and poor mind in the wisdom age, and be in unending super-abundance as follows:

1. Poor mind think impossibilities. The rich mind thinks possibilities. The poor always complain "I cannot do this" "I cannot do that" and "It cannot be done by any man". He expends his time precious energy to conjure up impossibilities in every task. But the rich mind sees differently. The rich mind sees ten ways it can be done and as well as ten ways it can be done under a different condition. The rich man is

quite rational in discerning and reasoning even if under intense stress.

2. The poor mind sees risk everywhere and avoids challenges. The rich mind sees opportunities and goes for them. Globalization streams with new vistas of opportunities across the globe while bearing in it's nestle varying pedigree of challenges. The poor mind only sees the challenges as difficulties or risks that must be avoidable, while the rich mind sees difficulties as challenges that serve as raw materials to process riches.

This way these two lead separate life styles.

3. The Poor mind gives reasons and excuses. The rich mind pursues results and performance. Excuses have never won recognition or excellent award anywhere, but performance if golden.

4. The poor mind thinks lack and limitations. The rich mind thinks prosperity and abundance, and he become prosperous because as a man thinks so he is". It is a universal code separating the poor from the rich of the land.

5.   The poor mind has wishes. The rich mind has purpose. Wishes are only horses in weird fantasy Island and beggars could fly to Buckingham palaces of this world. But in real life purpose is a commander of earthly riches.

6.   The poor mind withholds. The rich mind gives. Givers never lack because his hands is always atop the receiver's hand.

7.   The poor mind works for money to finance expenses. The rich mind

makes money work for him by investing it.

8. The poor mind sees problem as obstacles and a dead end. The rich mind sees problem as challenges and stepping stones to success.

9. The poor mind seeks for sympathy. The rich mind goes for empathy.

10. The poor mind is ungrateful. The rich mind is appreciative.

It is important to note here, that, the "lack-programming" of the mid brings financial cancer to the pocket. The reason that many capable people are poor is because they see themselves in terms of what they lack; lack of education, lack of a capital to start, lack of good family background, etc. In the wisdom age repackage your mind set with positive programming then, you surely re-invent your income.

"4 Steps to Achieve Money Multiplication in This Wisdom Age"

The Universe spins with power of multiplication and our part in life is to tap into this sample equation of life to enrich us. Whenever multiplication is involved, then other aspect of mathematics are involved also. Therefore, hence, I want to take you through four plan exercises to enable you to multiply your money as follows:

1. Factorization: If you must multiply your money without difficulty, first bring together all needs and challenges, then, factor out the most important or common variable that can impact seriously on your life. Invest money wisely in this area to gain the multiplicity of your fund in a mean time interval.

Ritchie Felix,
Copyright by Ritchie Felix

You do not need to do every business to grow your money. You do not need to invest your money in every portfolio to become financially independent, rather choose one out of the box that shows track-record of performance and invest your fund. The same thing goes for banking, you do not need to keep your money in all the banks around for its security, just choose one out of the multitude and save yourself a headache due to anxiety.

2. Addition: - This is the simplest form of mathematics that even a lunatic can handle any day. You must be focus and faithful to yourself and to your vision or mission to add all you can to your success in life. Add your intellectual prowess, your planning, your character, your network of associates, your persistence, your hard or smart work, capital and all that is necessary to make it happen for you.

It is important you do not add up your positives to your negatives to avoid achieving nothing at the end of the day. In recession, the richest people around utilizes this simplest format to ride on the wings of greatness. Your minus is either a challenge or an excuse that militates against your vision. Excuses are excuses but performance is golden to the world. The 21st century has no place for excuses but celebrates productivity, performance and success. So add up your values, your gift and talents to the above mentioned to en-route to money multiplication.

3. Subtraction: - Be discipline enough to subtract all known bad habits and friends that can mar your vision for success. Take away characteristic traits that can impair your focus and ditch your mission. Money multiplication cannot happen in the presence of laziness mixed with lack of confidence.

Take away debts and lack of commitment on your path to the vision before you. The richest, strongest and most influential people of the country took away several things off their pathway to success and prominence. It is a mortal responsibility that you owe to yourself. There is no power or external entity that does this for you, except you. Likewise there is no force strong enough to stop you in life except the one within you. You are the

The Sagacity of the Richest Man of the Century

The greatest import of the present age is the internet. The international network presents to the entire human race alive the opportunity to create uncommon impact on the sands of time of this generation. Little wonder, only very few people are really taking the bull by the horns to stay productive despite the global scale turmoil of varying pedigrees. These sages constitute the 20% of entire world population that controls the 80% of world resources. The richest people among this breed have discovered attitudes, skills and exceptional strategies for achieving greatness.

While the rest of the world basks in the euphoria of evolving information climate; the richest man of the century is busy processing this information to specialize knowledge that can put him ahead of the entire pack permanently. This is sagacious and unusual cleverness of a Sage. The richest man refused to get trapped by the tiara of information as the rest of the world. He understands the dynamism of innovative information when consciously processed to specialized knowledge quantum from which proceeds outstanding productivity and unmatchable performances respectively. The richest man has the eyes to decipher the gold in everything, especially in its raw state. This is uncommon with the ordinary people of the world. This is sure the vast chasm separating the poor from the rich people of the world.

Do you know that the information released on the internet daily will take a man 20 years to study and decode into various pedigree of usefulness. The world at present has so much information but lacks knowledge. Having just raw information about anything is not enough to crown you king in the market places and market spaces of the world. You have to process what you have into knowledge to address specific problem of man to swell your bank account with money. You have to learn the process extracting useful information from the information-bank of the world. Then, gain the mastery of turning it into goldmine. This way you get flush with superabundant money and roll yourself in great fortune.

There are billions of books, journals, tapes, graphics, newspapers, magazines, web logs, websites and audio materials where lots of information can be accessed, but only very few productive conscious people go a step further to decoding the quanta of specialized-knowledge locked in it. It is an aberration to have access to millions of information around and still live in penury. It cost you little or nothing to build up your own self knowledge that can culminate into an uncommon password to help you access the treasury without measure in-built in every iota of information that fly in the tiny air. This is exactly what the richest man of the century does to stay lush in wealth and roll in labyrinth of fortune. It is a principle every aspiring and ambitious fellow must posses in his kitty and wisely keep permanent at work all through his life.

The richest man of the world creates a definite plan to improve himself in both art of money making and "antics of money keeping". One major area that he is attracted to is where information can be found as he can make it useful for himself and the situations on hand. That is sublime sagacity of a Sage! You too can do same and stay on top of your world and command the wealth of afar countries with ease.

The richest man browses the search engines to know what people are looking for and get the statistical analysis of how many people looking for "this" or "that" and where these people are located. Then come out with an innovative import to satisfy these needs and swell his bank account, while the poor people browses the pages of websites to seek for luck or opportunity to invest their money and cash a miracle. Rarely do the poor meet their expectations online as there are many scam schemes waiting to happen in the super highway.

Ritchie Felix,
Copyright by Ritchie Felix

Trinity of riches

e) **Riches Are Within Your Reach**:
Until you come to see things around you
as money in its raw state you will hardly
live the life of your dream. You will not
be the man of your envious dream if you
cannot capture the portrait of the life you
want to lead where you are right now.
Your desire to drive the car of your
dream, marry wife of your dream and live
in the house of your dream in anchored
on your shoulders. You have what it
takes to lead, live the life of full of bliss

and roll in the superabundant of wealth. You are the cornucopia of wealth, just look deep inside within you and manifest enough outside to gain the power to unleash your treasure without measure to your world.

f) **Riches Have Their Beginning in Your Mind**: Wealth is state of the mind. It is a brain child of your consciousness. Riches begin to accumulate in your mind first as ideas and magnetized desires. One thing to do to give birth to your dream is to expand on your ideas, expand your magnetized thought pattern, update your knowledge and stretch your vision beyond the circumstances surrounding you at the moment. Then move from strategic thinking to genius thinking via habitual use of your mind telepathic activity. Grow the prosperity of your dream by rightly engaging your mind at work always.

g) **Riches start with understanding of your position in life**: Your foremost assignment on earth is to discover your true place on earth and not to struggle to get ahead of others around you. You have a distinct place on earth and it is golden if you discover it on time. You are designed originally by God to exploit the potentials of the earth and the ones sunk deep within you. You have to grow spiritually, physically and financially to lead the lifestyle you desire. It is a crime against humanity if you fail to discover your pristine position on earth.

The friends that will help you into your self-satisfying lifestyle are usually connected to the kind of money you make. Creativity starts between your two ears, two eyes, two legs, two nostrils and one mouth. This is a golden truth you must buy and keep all the days of your life on this planet.

The Truth about Money and Riches

a) **Power and Authority**: The truth about money is that, having it give you a kind of hope, confidence and might to do certain things that ordinarily you couldn't do. Having money will give you power and authority over your life to build up your own self knowledge and rule your world with great fortune. Money has a spirit that can give you the carriage and courage to face life challenges without fear of any uncertainty. To those who have money, they can face any impossibility that those who do not have it fears. People who lack money go through unprintable, deprivations, eerie and endless unsolvable problems.

b) **Foundation for livelihood**: The human existence in terms of food, clothes, shelter and whole lot of others depend on the foundation of money. Money gives a man the pedestal and velocity to move into his dream and vision for life. Money plays vital role in the upkeep of man and helps him achieve his purpose on the planet earth. To get education and good one at that you need to be very rich and also have the ability to stay rich. To fulfill religious obligations, get the best of comfort and relaxation, and healthy living for yourself and for anyone around you, money will play significant role for things to work. Money is the imperative and the password you need to prepare the foundation of your future and lead the lifestyle you want.

c) **Money is the god of this world:**
Apart from God in the Heaven, money is the second god of this world that influences everything we do in this world. You might not retain your wife even with her children if you lack money on the constant basis. You may lose your respect before your friends if you out of money for too long. You may lose your girl friend to your pals if you are not in money. Several marriages have hit the corridors of divorce on infidelity for lack of money on the side of the spouse. Money is very important in life and after life for those you left behind.

d) **Status symbol:** It is far better you have money than for you to lack it. Money give you're a status symbol in the society. There are levels of privileges that you will command if you money in abundance beyond the imagination of ordinary people in the society. You can hardly face same fate as the poor in most cases of life. You enjoy certain level of paparazzi from both government and individuals. Without money you cannot enjoy certain level of credit facilities from your bank.

e) **Riches Are Within Your Reach**:
Until you come to see things around you as money in its raw state you will hardly live the life of your dream. You will not be the man of your envious dream if you cannot capture the portrait of the life you want to lead where you are right now. Your desire to drive the car of your dream, marry wife of your dream and live in the house of your dream in anchored on your shoulders. You have what it takes to lead, live the life of full of bliss and roll in the superabundant of wealth. You are the cornucopian of wealth, just

look deep inside within you and manifest enough outside to gain the power to unleash your treasure without measure to your world.

f) Riches Have Their Beginning in Your Mind: Wealth is state of the mind. It is a brain child of your consciousness. Riches begin to accumulate in your mind first as ideas and magnetized desires. One thing to do to give birth to your dream is to expand on your ideas, expand your magnetized thought pattern, update your knowledge and stretch your vision beyond the circumstances surrounding you at the moment. Then move from strategic thinking to genius thinking via habitual use of your mind telepathic activity. Grow the prosperity of your dream by rightly engaging your mind at work always.

g) Discover Your True position on Earth: Your foremost assignment on earth is to discover your true place on earth and not to struggle to get ahead of others around you. You have a distinct place on earth and it is golden if you discover it on time. You are designed originally by God to exploit the potentials of the earth and the ones sunk deep within you. You have to grow spiritually, physically and financially to lead the lifestyle you desire. It is a crime against humanity if you fail to discover your pristine position on earth.

The friends that will help you into your self-satisfying lifestyle are usually connected to the kind of money you make. Creativity starts between your two ears, two eyes, two legs, two nostrils and one mouth. This is a golden truth you must buy and keep all the days of your life on this planet.

COMMON DENOMINATORS OF THOSE WHO GROW RICH in wisdom age that you need to know to rule in wealth

The principle of success works anywhere for anybody irrespective of size of status, status of education attainment, religious affiliation and gender department you belong. The principle of gravity demands that anything that goes up comes down irrespective of quantity or quality or even who throw it up in the first place. This is a universal principle and spins across the orbit of earth. The rich people of the universe have several common principles they share with each other no matter where they are located in the earth vast expansive space, and no matter what they engages their abilities and money to do.

The first fundamental denominator of those who grow rich is that:

❖ They spend much less than what they earn at a time:- It is great wisdom to save money for the rainy day which is certain to come. The rich people makes wise provisions for themselves by withholding some parts of their income at a time, and only spend on essential needs that cannot be avoided. The poor spends above his salary and probably accumulate debts to be serviced by his next month income. This way the poor go into financial slavery and penury for reckless spending.

The rich goes for profitable business negotiation before spending a dime out of his income, but the poor is driven to spend his hard earn income on mere sales pitch of smart salesmen. At long run, the Rich tie up a business deal even without a deposit of dime from his income, but the poor pays for everything he buys. The Rich will engage his acumen to harness the profits; advantage and leverages on the deal to roll in financial abundance, but the poor cannot get anything out of an already made product save instant satisfaction. To get this satisfaction again, he need to pay again and again, and this way the poor gets poorer and the Rich get richer.

The second fundamental denominator of those who grow rich is that:

❖ The rich spends from his profit: The rich spends from his profit to enrich him further, but the poor spends from his capital or from his earned income. The money in the rich man hands has way it multiplies its economic value by way of good investments in portfolios that continue to churn out profits even when the man is not present to facilitate thing to work. The poor sees only his pay check and what it can afford to deliver an instant gratification. The future is not usually factored into the equation of everyday life of the poor. So his income serves him as both capital and profit at same time. He only come to consciousness when the last time is spent on impulse buy, then, he goes back to turning the wheels to earn the next income. This is quite frustrating and wasting life style. The poor man way of living is expensive, dangerous and impoverishing in the whole.

Profit is not earned from working for another; it is the outcome of a business over time and time again. The Rich believes so much in profiteering –activities to attain financial independent, but the poor believes in so many activities to earn his income which by all standards is temporal and definite to a time discourse. Profit is a better leverage than earned income as it increases the value of the capital while expanding its options. Earned income can do same if properly invested to create an own business with good profit potentials. This way the poor can gradually transform his enormous liabilities into asset, and roll in money and basks in the euphoria of rich business contacts.

Chapter Eight

"IF YOU MUST BE PRODUCTIVE AND LIVE TO THE FULLEST OF YOUR LIFE, DEVELOP THESE 7 AREAS"

- **FINANCIAL AREA: -** What is your risk-taking-ability like? When last did you take a risky step towards upgrading your finances? What is your risk profile like? What level of financial freedom do you desire to reach? And what are you doing now to arrive at that? What do you know about Investment?

- **EDUCATIONAL/SELF IMPROVEMENT: -** In a world of books, readers are leaders. In a house of cards, players are golden treasures. What level of education do you desire to reach and why? What level of self improvement do you desire to achieve and why? You probably might not go too far to enjoy life in the 21st century if you lack education or fail to develop yourself up to the minute. You are

Ritchie Felix,
Copyright by Ritchie Felix

the architect of your fortune. You can write your own script and roll in great fortune. You can gain your future if you can build up your own self knowledge and make it your own modus operandi daily.

- **SPIRITUAL NEED:** - What is your belief about God? Do desire a relationship with Him? Or are an atheist? You have to be in constant touch with creator to accomplish your mission on earth. You have to know that without God, you can only do little despite all your lofty intelligence. You are a product of a manufacturer who brought you into existence without a purpose. He has your working manual and you need this to maximize your life full potentials. If you are enjoying a fulfilling relationship with your mother, you can start today.

- **WORK AREAS: -** It is important you draft up a plan about how long and how far you are going to put into civil service or into private sector working for another. Salary cannot make you gain financial independent, but working for yourself in your own business can with time. You have take stock of your skills, gift and talents, and seek to decipher your tool of best fit that can deliver your financial expectation within a short time frame. It is either you develop a new career while still keeping your present job. Or resign to strategize and start life afresh there is no distant too long to start afresh. What you need to start is a clear vision about what, where and how you choose to gain financial freedom. Switch your focus on this vision and be in the dream of your life.

- **HEALTH/RECREATIONAL AREAS:** - Health is greatest wealth of any people in life. Recreational activities are the only way to sustain good health. What are you introducing into your system that will support life and not deplete its values? Any harmful substance will somehow shorten your life span. You have to introduce into your system thing that will aid reinvigorate your health and keep your ever healthy at all time. Your good ideas, theories, great certificates from notable institutions and all that efflorescence you may generate requires a healthy body to carry it around. You have to register at the gym to keep fit and keep the soul prosperity via bodily exercises.

- **COMMUNITY AREAS:** - You are not an Island, so you surely come from somewhere- a community; you have to become part of the development force of your society by way of living and participating positively to impact upon others in the community. This way you have better and roll in great outcomes.

"RELIGIOUS VIEWS ABOUT MONEY & RICHES"

The background of any person or people is very important especially the religious background of any individual goes along way to affect his personal believe system, perspectives and attitude towards everything about life. There are real and unreal philosophies of thought or doctrines that flow with religious affiliations. Those who believe that the love of money or having it in excess, that is riches, is a sin- do not encourage its members to pursue after money or riches. Even if they have the opportunity to do so, for religious reasons, you see such fanatic abscond from such material pursuit.

However, on the contrary, - those who holds opposite view about money and riches, goes a long way to create cornucopia of wealth and roll in amazing fortune. The school of thoughts of life plays significant and fundamental role in determining our strategic positioning per time in regard to money making and accumulation of riches. It is this fact that every grown up adult need to check out to actually determine why he is going up or going down - economically in life.

MONEY VERSUS PRAYER: - Some religion teaches erroneous doctrines to their followers about money and prayer. There is this prevailing culture among some groups that prayer alone will make you get unlimited supply of money, and make you be in money. But when you watch their heads, they live in condors and bask in the euphoria of riches of all manners. From different currencies to material possessions of various magnificent status. Then, surprisely, you see all the ardent followers suffer in miserable poverty waiting for bread to fall from heaven into their plates to eat. This is great error that calls for immediate correction.

When God created the first man and woman; he commanded them to subdue the earth, dominate their world and multiply the earth with abundance.

He did not hand them over a prayer bulletin or manual with prayer points. Ignorance is the mother of all stagnant and primitive orthodoxy oozing from these altars of "holier than Maya"

From Genesis to the Revelation in the Holy Bible, prayer was mentioned 500 times, and money or riches was mentioned and referenced 2500 times. From this vantage point, it is easier and clearer to believe that 2500 times of worthy mentioning or reference to both money and riches depicts significant importance of the two to the Heavenly mandate given to the believers or the church. This underscores the fact that most wealthy empires of the world are controlled by Christians or Believers of the Gospel of Christ.

Similarly, same is applied to other religions that believe in money and riches. The Moslems believes in the unlimited supply of money and in the greatness of Allah-God to this. Likewise other religious groups. Little wonder, money is a sacred instrument that has been around for ages. It has been a major standard of measurement of effort, attainment and performance. If you have a wrong view or faculty perspective about money or riches, you will hardly come close to having it in abundance.

METAPHYSICAL VIEWS ABOUT MONEY AND RICHES

♦ **DEFINITION OF KEYWORD- METAPHYSICS:** - The word Metaphysics refers to the philosophy concerning the nature of existence, truth and knowledge. The Metaphysicians believe in God but not much in hard work. The fundamental perspective or preoccupation of a metaphysician is dealing with the philosophy of the mind. The Psychologist deals with the science of the mind. It is imperative to note that, these two branches of knowledge have the MIND as the prime object.

◆ **FUNDAMENTAL ACTIVITIES OF A METAPHYSICIAN: -** The mind is the crystal ball of the metaphysician with which he carries out his activities. He tests his hypothesis and hymosis within the frame work of the mind parlance. The mind is the hub of intellectual powers in man. The intellect is the faculty by which the mind receives and comprehends. The one who harness this power of the mind is an intellectual and he possesses the mental power to program or predict the mind capableness at any time. A Metaphysician possess the science of the mind which enables him to tap the telecosmic power of the mind and the applicable technicalities to heal to attract, to elevate, to do and undo a thing or circumstance as he ever wishes.

♦ **MONEY PERSPECTIVE OF A METAPHYSICIAN:-** The Metaphysician believes in unlimited supply of money and super-abundant riches of the cosmos that can be tapped by active engagement on the mind telecosmic magnetic power. This mental attitude makes the Metaphysician programs the mind to unleash its spiritual prowess, intelligence and functional wisdom to bring into reality whatever the convolutions of the mind could configure in its subconscious state. Note, the spiritual prowess here, is not the spiritual of the Holy Heavenly places, but of the lower level of the soul plane. The soul is the spirit man in the physical man. Remember, every human is a tripartite being having body, spirit and the soul to have plenteous money is material by the

Metaphysician and do not have anything to do with Heaven or Hell.

THERE ARE TWO TYPES OF METAPHYSICIANS IN THE WORLD, NAMELY:-

a. **PRACTIONERS**

b. **NON-PRACTIONERS**

The Practioners are those who utilize the brain power of man to attract riches and fortune for either themselves or others who are clients. This class of Metaphysician believes so much in God just as the non-practioners, but do not believe so much in physical exertion to make money or accumulate riches.

The practioners are usually found in their worship places like the Church, Personal altar or apartment. The non-practioners are usually big business moguls, financial gurus, celebrities, inventors, sports men and women, and etc, who utilize the mental power to recreate their own world of abundance, fortune and greatness. These men and women are in minority in every society, and are usually CEOs or Managers of Companies or even owners of corporate ladder that uses other people brain to make his money.

Mental power is superior to the crude energy dissipation.

"SOCIOLOGICAL VIEW ABOUT MONEY & RICHES"

- **PERSPECTIVE OF MONEY:-** In the social cycles or society money is simply a paper printed and metallic coins manufactured at the government approval as the standard measure of payment as the buyer and seller could us it to fathom quantity or quality of product or service rendered, and as a means for procurements. Though, it is only but paper or metallic coin, the value conferred upon it gives a status of authority and legitimacy to be generally accepted by all as medium of exchange, and means of settlement of indebtedness. Every other paper or materials made of same raw materials do not have same value.

♦ **FUNDAMENTAL CHARACTERISTICS OF SOCIALOGICAL MONEY: -** In the ancient world, we heard of trade by barter where goods were exchange goods or service. At some time, cowries, firewood, slaves, salt, sheep, oxen, farm yields, etc were used as means of exchange. This level of money somehow affected the minds of individual in both concept and perspective about this view of money. As civilization brought about the present day money controlled by Central Authority the government. The Government decides the – colour, design, size, quality and quantity of money that would be in use in the society at any given time.

Generally, good money anywhere must have the following characteristics features:

♦ **Uniformity**
♦ **Divisibility**

- **Easily recognizable**
- **Portability**
- **Durability**
- **Acceptability**
- **legality**

- **MONEY DISTRIBUTION IN THE SOCIETY:-**Money is distributed in the society base on several factors ranging from tangible to intangibles as accepted by all as norms and values of the societal culture. To access greater fund in the corporate security you need to have more degrees and occupy higher position ahead of others. The government share money to citizens as wages for work or service rendered. You get more money depending on the quality of service you renders to either the government enterprise or private enterprise. Positioning of office or appointment into service is base on education attainment or paper certificate obtained from high institution. This made the era of industrial revolution swell with more men and women scavenging for higher degrees in various institutions of learning across the globe.

To accumulate excess money which is riches, you need to work very hard to earn prominent position or office in the society to make much money and work less in service time. Other ways available to get more money includes buying of stocks, government securities and bonds, trading on the platform of foreign exchange and investment into pyramid scheme with an own product. These channels have provided opportunities for citizens of society to accumulate huge fund in their treasury or bank account to become very rich. It is surprising, that, this is the defunct working mentality of all in the society towards making excess money, except for few who generates from a different economic paradigm reality.

It is important to note here that, God or His care agency is not responsible for money- distribution in the society because God originally did not create money rather money is the brain child of man. The principle governing its acquisition and accumulation was also framed by man. You apply the principle you get results accordingly.

"PHILOSOPHICAL VIEWS ABOUT MONEY AND RICHES"

♦ **WORK HARD TO EARN MONEY:**

- North-South, East-West, hard

work is never separated from making money and making it in abundant. Just some way is a norm to use the mental power to create wealth among the metaphysicians-hard work is a common belief standard in every society to enable individual earn money and earn enough of it. That is to say, the better your hard work, the more your chances to make extra cash and roll in fortune. The Christians, Moslems and several other religious bodies believe that nothing is wrong with actual hardworking to earn a living, even though part of their teaching cum tenet emphasizes that hard work is not a precursor of blessing, that is, earning wealth or good living.

♦ **GOD BLESSES AND NOT HARD WORK:-** The Christian faithful of the world believe that riches do not come to everybody, especially, those who strives to work harder than others, but comes to those Heaven has destined to have excess riches. The common believe in this cycle is that God is responsible to bless his children with money and give it to them in abundance the way of hard work. Even Moslem faithfuls shows philosophy about making money and amazing great wealth. This way the Priest and Prophet do not work to earn money. The Iman in Islam do not work to earn a living. Every other person can work and work very hard, then, trust God – Allah to bless his effort to yield great results (i.e. financial and material results)

Little wonder, the Africans seems to work much harder than any people on the face of earth, but often came out with less desired results in terms of finances and materiality respectively. I make haste to submit that money and riches are both influenced by the religious philosophy of any people about it. This is measurable and reliable as a standard to relate it with levels of development of any society. The African continent is known for multi-religious affiliation of her people which has often time caused dispute, hostility, and even triggered civil wars. There are sects that do not believe in education or call it western education. Others do not believe in making via investment in breweries that brews alcohol drinks or beverages.

You do not expect such people to eke out living by the

means that strongly agitate against their personal belief, hence, the chances for them to create wealth even if given the opportunity is not exploited. Christian faithfuls are not ready to own stocks in printing press that only churn out occultic books no matter the magnitude of its profit quotient. The same applies to other religious across the region. This way wealth creation is perceive from multidimensional screens of religious prism which tends to determine how each believer amasses his wealth from vast resources of the earth.

- **GRACE OF GOD VERSUS HARDWORK:** - Grace is the unmerited favour of God on a man. Some people believe that no matter how much you try or prepare to try through hard work, you may not get at anything worthwhile. That God Divine Grace is the only that empowers a man, and determine who should be rich or poor. Even, this teaching or submission according to many people have its root on the scripture in the Bible where God said "I will show mercy on whom I choose to show mercy" it all boil down to what an individual believe as his own legitimate means of earning living.

"THE LAST TWO HABITS OF THE POOR THAT MAKES THEM MISERABLE POOR AND STRANDED IN LIFE"

♦ Much has been written by people about the seven habits of most effective people of the world. Also, much have been written about the seven habits of the poor that makes them very poor which the richest people avoided to swim In unlimited supply of money and super-abundance. I strongly believe that several people out there will like to know much more about the habits that make one bath in poverty and live in poverty all through life time despite the fact, several others we like to call fortunate people keeping plundering the cornucopian of wealth of the cosmos. The 8th habit of the poor that makes them miserable poor and stranded in life expands into two hub as follows:-

a. **LACK OF ADEQUATE RIGHT MENTAL PROGRAMMING:** - Just too many miserable people of the world lack adequate mental programming in the right information or body of knowledge to get out of poverty. to some this disaster happen unconsciously while to many others, it is a question of belief system. You cannot separate a man future from his present belief system and culture of values. There are people under demonic hypnosis that they cannot profit from any business venture. This is wrong foundation in the realm of the Spiritual that can render such life forever useless on earth. To help people in this bracket out of miserable poverty, you have to first discover the misconception within and de-bug the mind of its effect before reprogramming the mind with useful information and knowledge scheme. There are others who grew up in a world of myths and superstitions belief about everything in life. This is a wrong mind programming that can crash all hopes and renders the individual in quote helpless in a precarious situation. I have a friend or rather a student right now undergoing my mentorship program whose Parents etched into the convolution of his brain from cradle that has planned everything about living a good life on earth for him, so needless struggling or even working to earn this by himself. He had believed on this till now he is 25yrs, his condition keep getting worse by every minute of the day. He went through the secondary and higher institution with this obnoxious mindset, and he is stucked in impoverish poverty. His parent's condition is not getting better either. Their mystical approach to life have turned out Chains of misery and confined them to prison of hopelessness. This is what lack of adequate right mind programming can do to any person or people anywhere in the world.

b. **LACK OF ADEQUATE ACTION:-**

Naturally, everything on the earth surface has the ability to escape into the space if given the required escape for velocity according to Sir Isaac Newton's laws of motion. Consequently, there are levels of riches you cannot attain in life until you give yourself and life the needed conscious action targeted enough to push over the edge of stardom. The rich people of the world know exactly this significant principle that input of adequate action into any system or process brings about corresponding but opposite reaction.

Ritchie Felix,
Copyright by Ritchie Felix

The poor lack this uncommon poise and fire to launch him into the world of financial freedom. Most poor knew all the dynamics and mechanics involve in getting unlimited supply of money, but somehow feel reluctant to attempt using it to their advantage. This way they sink gradually but surely into miserable poverty and get stranded in life.